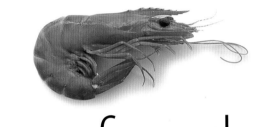

seafood

Produced by **ACP**books

Printed by Bookbuilders, China.
Published by ACP Publishing Pty Limited, 54 Park Street, Sydney, NSW 2000 (GPO Box 4088, Sydney, NSW 2001),
phone (02) 9282 8618, fax (02) 9267 9438, www.acpbooks.com.au
AUSTRALIA: Distributed by Network Services, GPO Box 4088, Sydney, NSW 2001, phone (02) 9282 8777, fax (02) 9264 3278.
UNITED KINGDOM: Distributed by Australian Consolidated Press (UK), Moulton Park Business Centre, Red House Road,
Moulton Park, Northampton, NN3 6AQ, phone (01604) 497 531, fax (01604) 497 533, acpukltd@aol.com
CANADA: Distributed by Whitecap Books Ltd, 351 Lynn Avenue, North Vancouver, BC, V7J 2C4,
phone (604) 980 9852, fax (604) 980 8197, customerservice@whitecap.ca www.whitecap.ca
NEW ZEALAND: Distributed by Netlink Distribution Company, ACP Media Centre, Cnr Fanshawe and Beaumont Streets,
Westhaven, Auckland (PO Box 47906, Ponsonby, Auckland, NZ), phone (09) 366 9966, ask@ndcnz.co.nz

Gourmet Seafood.
Includes index.
ISBN 1 86396 369 3.
1. Cookery (Seafood). 2. Cookery (Fish). I. Title. II. Title: Australian Gourmet Traveller.
641.692
© ACP Publishing Pty Limited 2004
ABN 18 053 273 546
Front cover: Seafood paella with alioli, page 70.

AUSTRALIAN GOURMET TRAVELLER
Group publisher Phil Scott
Editorial director Andy Harris
Creative director Emma Ross
Editor Anthea Loucas
Food department Sophia Young,
Christine Osmond, Kathleen Gandy

ACP BOOKS
Editorial director Susan Tomnay
Creative director & designer Hieu Chi Nguyen
Senior editor Julie Collard
Publishing manager (sales) Brian Cearnes
Publishing manager (rights & new projects) Jane Hazell
Brand manager Donna Gianniotis
Production manager Carol Currie
Business manager Seymour Cohen
Assistant business analyst Martin Howes
Studio manager Caryl Wiggins
Pre-press Harry Palmer
Editorial & sales coordinator Caroline Lowry
Editorial assistant Karen Lai

Photographer Ian Wallace
Stylist Amber Keller
Food editor Leanne Kitchen
Recipes by Vanessa Broadfoot, Bronwen Clark,
Kathleen Gandy, Leanne Kitchen, Lynne Mullins,
Christine Osmond, Kathy Snowball, Sophia Young
Food preparation by Christine Sheppard

Chief executive officer John Alexander
Group publisher Pat Ingram
Publisher Sue Wannan

THANKS TO THESE STOCKISTS AND SUPPLIERS
All Hand Made, phone (02) 9386 4099
The Art of Tiles, phone (02) 9565 1066
Bison Homewares, phone (02) 6284 2334
The Ceramic Shed, phone (02) 4627 9651
Mud Australia, phone (02) 9518 0220
Murdoch Produce, phone (02) 9517 9499
Stem, phone (02) 9810 5222

With special thanks to Demcos Seafoods, phone (02) 9700 9000

AUSTRALIAN GOURMET TRAVELLER

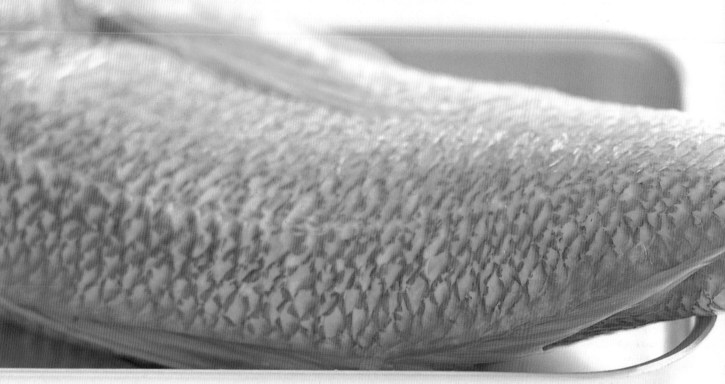

seafood

ACPbooks

contents

COOKING TECHNIQUES

The most important rule to observe when cooking seafood is not to overcook it, as it becomes dry and tough very easily. Once you remove the fish from the heat source it will continue to cook because of the residual heat, so if it appears a little underdone, stand in a warm place to "rest" for 5-10 minutes by which time it should be cooked through. To ascertain if fish is cooked, gently pry a small piece of flesh with a fork and if flesh comes away easily and is opaque, the fish is done. However, some fish such as salmon, swordfish, kingfish and tuna are best cooked rare to medium-rare. Use recipe cooking times only as a guide, as the thickness of fish fillets varies significantly and cooking times should be adjusted accordingly.

PAN-FRYING

A heavy-based frying pan is essential for pan-frying seafood, to ensure the heat is maintained during cooking and evenly distributed. For thick fillets of fish, use an ovenproof frying pan so you can finish the cooking in the oven to avoid over-browning on the outside.

When pan-frying fish with the skin on, first place the fish, skin-side down, in a very hot non-stick frying pan and press with a spatula so skin crisps evenly. Do not attempt to move fish until it does so freely when you shake the pan, otherwise skin will stick to base of pan.

When cooking large quantities of seafood, such as scallops or squid, make sure you don't overcrowd pan or seafood will stew rather than sear. Cook in small batches only, allowing pan to get very hot before adding next batch to pan.

BARBECUING AND CHAR-GRILLING

Similarly to pan-frying, seafood should be cooked on a very hot, lightly oiled pre-heated barbecue or char-grill and cooked until a light golden crust forms on one side before turning, to prevent sticking. Drain marinades well to prevent flames from singeing the seafood. Wrapping seafood in foil or baking paper is an ideal way to cook tender-fleshed fish, which can be prone to falling apart when char-grilled or barbecued. Seal foil or paper tightly to preserve the delicious juices.

DEEP-FRYING

Use clean oil with a high smoking point, such as peanut or canola oil. If frying with coatings such as batter or breadcrumbs, remove cooked pieces after each batch or they will continue to cook and burn.

Don't attempt to cook other foods in the same oil you have cooked the seafood in, such as chips or sweet fritters, because the seafood flavour significantly permeates the oil. Keep a tray lined with crumpled absorbent paper right next to the deep-fryer; place deep-fried foods directly onto this tray so excess fat is absorbed immediately. Sprinkling fried foods with a little sea salt also helps maintain a crisp coating.

STIR-FRYING

This method is suited to crustaceans, clams, mussels, scallops, squid and firm-fleshed fish. Avoid cooking with oils that have a very low smoking point, such as sesame oil, as they will burn before the wok is hot enough to successfully stir-fry.

Cook seafood over high heat in small batches to prevent the temperature from dropping and seafood from stewing. If you are considering buying a wok, avoid electric woks – these don't provide sufficient heat for successful stir-frying. The best woks are made from carbon steel; these conduct heat well, improve with use and are non-reactive – unlike aluminium and cast iron. A wok with a non-stick surface may not be a good choice, as the coating can wear away over time; a good wok will have non-stick qualities anyway once seasoned with use.

pan-frying

barbecuing and char-grilling

deep-frying

stir-frying

baking

braising and stewing

poaching

steaming

BAKING

This method is best suited to whole fish, but also works well with fillets, shellfish or squid which can be baked on or layered with vegetables and a little oil, stock or wine to keep the seafood moist. Wrapping fish in foil or baking *en papillote* (wrapped in paper) is a great way of preserving the delicious juices. The addition of a little vermouth, wine or stock, a knob of butter and sprigs of thyme, marjoram or dill to the parcel makes a wonderfully fragrant sauce to pour over the fish once cooked. Baking whole fish in salt is another way of sealing in moisture. If baking seafood with vegetables, you will need to par-cook the vegetables before adding the seafood, or use vegetables such as radicchio and fennel which will generally cook in the same time as the seafood.

BRAISING AND STEWING

This long gentle cooking method is best suited to octopus and squid, although the terms "stew" and "braise" are often used very loosely to describe recipes in which firm-fleshed fish, molluscs or shellfish are added near the end of cooking. If braising or stewing on the stovetop, a simmer mat and heavy-based saucepan or casserole are very useful for helping keep the temperature very low and the braising or simmering liquid from boiling too rapidly.

POACHING

Best suited to whole or filleted firm-fleshed fish, poaching liquids include milk, olive oil, court bouillon, stock or water infused with aromatics. For large whole fish, start in cold liquid and bring up to a gentle heat, and for smaller fish and fillets start in warm liquid. Poaching liquid should only just be moving on the surface while cooking fish, and never simmering or boiling. Remove fish immediately from poaching liquid to prevent it from continuing to cook, then drain well before serving. Poaching a large whole fish is perfect for large crowds or dinner parties since they are ideal served at room temperature and can be done ahead. Fish poachers are necessary for poaching large whole fish, but small fish or fillets can be poached in a heavy-based frying pan or saucepan.

STEAMING

Best suited to molluscs such as mussels or oysters in the half shell and fish with delicate flesh. Steam molluscs in small batches, in a single layer, in a tightly sealed saucepan or wok, and remove as soon as shells open to prevent meat from overcooking and becoming tough and rubbery. Aromatics such as ginger, garlic, chilli, peppercorns, lemongrass and pungent herbs and citrus can be stuffed inside whole fish or scattered over before steaming to impart a delicate flavour. Individual bamboo steamers are ideal for steaming small fish or fillets; line with banana leaves and serve fish in the steamers.

Couscous is one of the many ingredients that found their way into the Sicilian repertoire as a result of Arab invasions hundreds of years ago.

Sicilian-style seafood couscous with lobster

2 tablespoons olive oil

1 onion, halved and thinly sliced

1 bulb of fennel, trimmed and thinly sliced

1 stalk of celery, finely chopped

1 small carrot, finely chopped

2 cloves of garlic, finely chopped

¼ teaspoon dried chilli flakes, or to taste

¼ teaspoon saffron threads, roasted and crumbled

1 litre fish or chicken stock

250ml dry white wine

1½ tablespoons tomato paste

2 fresh bay leaves

½ teaspoon dried Greek oregano

600g clams (vongole), soaked in cold water and drained

600g baby squid, cleaned and tentacles reserved, hoods cut into 1cm-wide strips

2 cooked lobsters (about 700g each), heads discarded, tails cut with shell into 5cm pieces

60g butter, chopped

400g (2 cups) instant couscous

Heat olive oil in a large heavy-based frying pan with a lid, then add onion, fennel, celery and carrot and cook over low heat for 8-10 minutes or until vegetables are soft but not brown. Add garlic, chilli flakes and saffron and cook for another 30 seconds or until fragrant. Add 2 cups stock, wine, tomato paste and herbs, bring to the boil, season to taste with sea salt and freshly ground black pepper, then simmer over low heat for 15 minutes. Add clams and cook, covered, for 5 minutes or until shells open, then add squid and lobster and cook for another 1-2 minutes or until just heated through.

Meanwhile, place remaining stock in a saucepan and bring to the boil. Add butter and couscous, season to taste and stand, covered, for 10 minutes, then fluff with a fork.

To serve, divide couscous among 6 shallow bowls, top with seafood, then ladle a little stock over and serve immediately.

Serves 6

Tony Tan's seafood laksa

Tony Tan is a Malaysian-born Melbourne chef and food historian. This is his
basic laksa recipe, which works very well with a variety of seafood. If candlenuts
are not available, blanched almonds or macadamias can be substituted.
A good-quality purchased laksa paste can be substituted for the spice paste.

⅓ cup olive oil

400ml coconut milk

1 tablespoon caster sugar

800ml fish or chicken stock

2 sprigs of Vietnamese mint

400g firm white fish fillets such as snapper
or mahi mahi

2 small squid, cleaned and sliced into rings

8 small black mussels, scrubbed and bearded

8 medium green prawns, peeled and cleaned
leaving tails intact

500g hokkien noodles, cooked in boiling
water for 1 minute, then drained

250g baby green beans, blanched in boiling
salted water for 30 seconds, then drained

Coriander sprigs and lime wedges, to serve

SPICE PASTE

2 stalks of lemongrass, outer layer removed,
root ends trimmed and stalks finely chopped

2 cloves of garlic, chopped

1 teaspoon ground turmeric or 3cm piece of
fresh turmeric, peeled and chopped

2.5cm piece of galangal, peeled and chopped

3cm piece of ginger, peeled and chopped

5 candlenuts

1 onion, chopped

6 fresh long red chillies or a mixture of
large and small chillies, chopped

2 teaspoons ground coriander

1 teaspoon roasted shrimp paste (belacan)

For spice paste, process all ingredients in a food processor
until a paste forms, adding a little water if necessary.

Heat oil in a large saucepan, add spice paste and cook,
stirring frequently, over medium heat for 5 minutes, or until
fragrant. Add coconut milk, sugar, stock and mint and, stirring
continuously, bring to the boil, then immediately reduce heat
to low and simmer for 15-20 minutes.

Add seafood to hot laksa stock and cook, covered, for
4-5 minutes or until seafood is just cooked and mussels open.
Divide noodles and green beans among 4 soup bowls then,
using a slotted spoon, top with seafood. Ladle hot stock over,
sprinkle with coriander sprigs and serve immediately with
lime wedges, passed separately.

Serves 4

Ideally, dried beans should be from the previous year's harvest, but as this is difficult to ascertain, purchase from continental delicatessens or other shops where the turnover is likely to be high.

Prawn, barley and bean soup

¼ cup olive oil

1 onion, finely chopped

2 cloves of garlic, thinly sliced

1 large carrot, finely chopped

3 stalks of celery, peeled
and finely chopped

2 dried bay leaves

100g (½ cup) dried cannellini beans,
soaked overnight, then drained

100g (½ cup) dried borlotti beans,
soaked overnight, then drained

100g (½ cup) dried chickpeas,
soaked overnight, then drained

2 litres fish or vegetable stock

65g (⅓ cup) pearl barley

1.2kg medium green king prawns,
cleaned, peeled and coarsely chopped

2½ tablespoons lemon juice, or to taste

½ cup coarsely chopped flat-leaf parsley

Extra virgin olive oil, to serve

Heat olive oil in a large saucepan, add onion, garlic, carrot and celery and stir over medium heat for 8 minutes or until vegetables are soft. Add bay leaves, drained beans and chickpeas and stock, bring mixture to a simmer, skimming surface regularly, and cook for 35 minutes or until beans and chickpeas are half cooked. Add pearl barley and cook for another 30 minutes or until beans, chickpeas and barley are tender. Stir in prawns and lemon juice, season to taste with sea salt and freshly ground black pepper, then simmer gently until prawns are just cooked. Stir in parsley, then divide soup among warm bowls and serve drizzled with a little extra virgin olive oil.

Serves 6-8

Chilled rocket and buttermilk soup with crabmeat

Extra virgin olive oil

1 large leek, white part only,
finely chopped

2 small sebago potatoes (about 500g),
chopped

3 cups chicken stock

2 bunches of rocket (about 400g), trimmed

300ml buttermilk

225g cooked blue swimmer or spanner
crab meat, picked through

2 Lebanese cucumbers, peeled, seeded
and cut into julienne

Heat 1½ tablespoons olive oil in a saucepan, add leek, potatoes and
1 teaspoon salt and cook over medium heat, stirring occasionally,
for 5-8 minutes or until leek is soft. Add stock and cook for another
20 minutes or until potatoes are soft. Cool slightly.

Meanwhile, cook rocket in boiling water for 1 minute or until wilted,
drain, then refresh in iced water and drain again. Squeeze excess
water from rocket and chop finely, then add to potato mixture.
Process mixture, in batches, in a food processor or blender until
smooth, then strain through a fine sieve into a bowl. Stir in buttermilk
and season to taste with sea salt and freshly ground black pepper,
then refrigerate until chilled. If soup thickens too much on cooling,
thin with a little extra buttermilk or chicken stock until desired
consistency is achieved.

Ladle into 6 small soup bowls, top with a little crabmeat
and cucumber and serve immediately.

Serves 6

Traditionally, buttermilk was the
liquid byproduct of the butter-making
process. Today, cultures are added
to low-fat milk, resulting in a slightly
thickened consistency and refreshing,
tangy taste.

Bourride

This rich, creamy soup is traditionally served in France as two courses – the aïoli-enriched stock as a soup, and the poached fish as a second course, served with extra aïoli. However, the bourride can also be eaten with both components combined; boiled potatoes and a simple green salad are the only accompaniments necessary.

2kg fish fillets (a mixture of snapper, blue-eye trevalla and ocean trout or salmon), skinned and pin-boned

8 egg yolks, lightly beaten

1 bunch of chives, finely chopped

FISH STOCK

2 tablespoons olive oil

1 onion, sliced

1 leek, sliced

2 carrots, sliced

2 sprigs of thyme

1 teaspoon fennel seeds

1 dried bay leaf

2cm-wide strip of orange rind

1.5kg white fish bones, rinsed and coarsely chopped

300ml dry white wine

AIOLI

4 egg yolks

1½ tablespoons Dijon mustard

2 tablespoons lemon juice, or to taste

6 cloves of garlic, finely chopped

400ml olive oil

For fish stock, heat olive oil in a large saucepan, add onion, leek, carrots, thyme, fennel seeds, bay leaf and orange rind and stir over low-medium heat for 5 minutes or until vegetables soften slightly. Add fish bones and stir over medium heat for 2 minutes, add wine and bring to the boil, then add enough water to just cover bones and vegetables. Bring mixture slowly to the boil, then reduce heat to low and simmer gently for 20 minutes, skimming surface regularly. Strain mixture, discarding solids.

For aïoli, process egg yolks, mustard, lemon juice and garlic in a food processor until smooth, then, with motor running, add olive oil in a slow, steady stream. Season to taste with sea salt and freshly ground black pepper and add more lemon juice if desired. Thin slightly with a little hot water, if necessary. Cover aïoli closely with plastic wrap, then refrigerate until needed.

Cut fish into 4-5cm pieces, then season to taste. Bring 1 litre fish stock to a simmer in a large saucepan (reserve remaining stock for another use), add fish and cook over low heat for 5 minutes or until just cooked. Remove from heat and, using a slotted spoon, transfer fish to a large plate or bowl, cover and set aside.

Whisk together egg yolks, 1 cup aïoli and ½ cup hot fish stock in a bowl until smooth; reserve remaining aïoli to pass separately or for another use. Add mixture to stock in pan, then stir continuously over low-medium heat until mixture thickens enough to coat the back of spoon; do not boil. Gently stir cooked fish and chives into soup, season to taste and serve immediately divided among 8 warm bowls, with extra aïoli passed separately, if using.

Serves 8

Pineapple features in Cambodian cuisine as an integral ingredient in the range of sour and sweet soups known as samlaa. The combination of tamarind, palm sugar and pineapple provides a delicate balance between these two vital elements of taste in South-East Asian cuisines.

Cambodian fish, pineapple and tomato soup

2 tablespoons tamarind purée

1.5 litres fish stock

2 tablespoons fish sauce

1 tablespoon grated palm sugar

4 stalks of lemongrass, white part only, bruised

3 cloves of garlic, bruised

800g gold band snapper, red emperor or coral trout fillets, skinned, pin-boned and cut into bite-size pieces

550g pineapple (about ¼ large), peeled, cored and chopped

1 vine-ripened tomato, cut into thin wedges

2 fresh red birdseye chillies, thinly sliced

2 tablespoons lime juice

2 tablespoons Vietnamese mint leaves, torn if large

2 tablespoons coriander sprigs

Lime wedges, Vietnamese mint leaves, round mint leaves and steamed jasmine rice, optional, to serve

Combine tamarind purée with 2 tablespoons water, then place in a large heavy-based saucepan or stockpot with stock, fish sauce, palm sugar, lemongrass and garlic, bring to the boil, then simmer for 10 minutes. Add fish and pineapple and cook for 3 minutes or until cooked through, then add tomato, chillies and lime juice and cook for another minute or until tomato is just soft. Remove from heat, stir in herbs, then serve immediately with lime wedges and mint leaves passed separately and steamed jasmine rice, if using.

Serves 4

Cream of cauliflower soup with oysters and parsley cream

40g butter

2 onions, finely chopped

1 head of cauliflower (about 1.5kg),
trimmed and cut into florets

1 fresh bay leaf

800ml milk

12 freshly shucked Sydney rock oysters,
removed from shell, juices reserved

Crusty bread, optional, to serve

PARSLEY CREAM

2 cups (firmly packed) flat-leaf
parsley leaves

300ml pouring cream

Melt butter in a heavy-based saucepan, add onions and cook over low heat for 6-8 minutes or until soft but not brown. Add cauliflower, bay leaf and milk and simmer over low heat for 25 minutes or until cauliflower is very tender. Remove bay leaf, process mixture in a food processor until smooth, then strain through a fine sieve into a clean pan.

Meanwhile, for parsley cream, place parsley in a heatproof bowl, cover with boiling water and stand for 1 minute. Drain and refresh parsley leaves in iced water, then drain again and squeeze excess moisture from parsley. Place cream in a large saucepan and simmer over low heat for 6-8 minutes or until reduced to 200ml. Blend parsley and 2 tablespoons hot cream in a blender until smooth, then add remaining cream and blend until well combined. Strain parsley cream through a fine sieve, then season to taste with sea salt and freshly ground black pepper, cover and refrigerate until needed.

Strain reserved oyster liquid through a fine sieve into cauliflower soup, then season soup to taste and stir over low heat until warmed through. Ladle soup among 4 warm bowls and top with a spoonful of parsley cream, then divide oysters among bowls and serve immediately, with crusty bread, if using.

Serves 4

The Sydney rock oyster is native to the estuaries of the eastern coast of Australia. If you do not plan to shuck your own oysters, ask your fishmonger to shuck them to order, reserving any juices.

Tomato, red capsicum and fish soup

Aged balsamic vinegar is a fragrant, sweetish vinegar from Modena, Italy, made from concentrated grape juice and aged in wooden barrels for at least 10 years.

2kg egg tomatoes, chopped

2 red capsicum, quartered and seeded

200g fennel (about ½ bulb), chopped

1 small carrot, finely chopped

2 heads of garlic, cloves separated, unpeeled

¼ cup extra virgin olive oil, plus extra, to serve

125ml dry white wine

1 tablespoon aged balsamic vinegar

2 cups fish stock, approximately

2 fresh bay leaves

600g monkfish (stargazer), whiting or flathead fillets, skinned, pin-boned and cut into bite-size pieces

GARLIC TOAST

1 small sourdough baguette, cut on the diagonal into 1cm-thick slices

Olive oil

Place vegetables and unpeeled garlic cloves in a roasting pan, drizzle with extra virgin olive oil, wine and balsamic vinegar, then cover with foil and roast at 200C for 1½ hours or until vegetables and garlic are tender, then remove foil and cook for another 30 minutes. Cool vegetables slightly, then peel capsicum and squeeze garlic from 8 cloves, reserving remaining garlic. Process vegetables, squeezed garlic and cooking liquid in a food processor until a smooth purée forms, then transfer to a large heavy-based saucepan.

Place stock, bay leaves and ½ teaspoon sea salt in another saucepan, bring to the boil and simmer for 10 minutes, then strain. Add strained stock to pan with purée, bring to the boil, then add fish, reduce heat to low and cook, covered for 5 minutes or until fish is just tender. Season to taste with sea salt and freshly ground black pepper.

For garlic toast, brush sliced sourdough with olive oil, then char-grill, on both sides, until golden and crisp. Squeeze 2 cloves of remaining roasted garlic onto each slice of grilled bread and spread slightly.

Ladle soup among 4 warm bowls and serve immediately with garlic toast to the side.

Serves 4

Steamed oysters with black bean dressing and noodle salad

2 tablespoons grapeseed oil

2 teaspoons finely grated ginger

1 clove of garlic, finely chopped

2 green onions, finely chopped

2 teaspoons drained salted black beans in soy sauce, rinsed and chopped

2 tablespoons Shaoxing wine

1 teaspoon sesame oil

12 freshly shucked Pacific oysters

NOODLE SALAD

100g fresh thin egg noodles

1 teaspoon sesame oil

2 tablespoons grapeseed oil

1 tablespoon chopped garlic chives

1 small Lebanese cucumber, seeded and cut into julienne

2 green onions, cut into julienne

2 tablespoons toasted sesame seeds

For noodle salad, cook egg noodles in boiling salted water for 3-5 minutes or until tender, drain and toss with oils, then cool slightly. Add remaining ingredients, then season to taste with sea salt and freshly ground black pepper and combine well.

Heat grapeseed oil in a small saucepan, add ginger, garlic and green onions and cook for 1 minute, then add black beans, wine and sesame oil and stir until heated through.

Place oysters in the top of a large bamboo steamer, spoon dressing over oysters, cover and cook over a wok of simmering water for 2-3 minutes or until just warmed through. Serve immediately with noodle salad to the side.

Serves 4

Salted black beans are black soya beans that have been fermented and preserved by salting. If soya beans in soy sauce are unavailable, substitute with those canned in brine or packaged in cryovac – purchase from Asian food stores.

Mace is the dried outer membrane of the nutmeg seed, and is available whole, in blades, or ground. Mace and seafood make a classic pairing.

Potted crab

350g cultured butter
350g cooked blue swimmer or spanner crab meat, picked through
Pinch of ground mace
¼ teaspoon cayenne
1 tablespoon lemon juice, or to taste
Melba toasts, to serve

Melt 200g butter, cool, then combine half the cooled melted butter with crab, spices and lemon juice. Season to taste with sea salt and freshly ground black pepper, then firmly pack mixture into four ¾-cup-capacity ovenproof dishes or one 3-cup-capacity ovenproof dish and place in a baking dish. Pour remaining cooled melted butter over crab, then pour enough boiling water into baking dish to come halfway up sides of dishes and cook at 150C for 25 minutes. Remove dishes from baking dish, cool to room temperature, then cover and refrigerate until cold.

Melt remaining butter in a small saucepan over low heat and simmer gently for 6-8 minutes or until white solids separate from butter. Do not brown. Pour clarified butter into a jug, leaving behind white solids, then stand until cool but not solidified. Pour enough cooled clarified butter over each dish to cover crab mixture, then refrigerate crab for 1 hour or until butter is firm. Serve potted crab with melba toasts.

Potted crab will keep refrigerated for up to 3 days.

Serves 8

Pickled octopus

2kg cleaned octopus (about 4 medium)
1 cup red wine vinegar
5 sprigs of dried Greek oregano
3 cloves of garlic, bruised
Large pinch of dried chilli flakes
¾ cup extra virgin olive oil
Kalamata olives and ouzo, optional, to serve

Combine octopus, ¼ cup red wine vinegar and oregano in
a large saucepan, cover and cook over low-medium heat for
1½ hours or until octopus is tender and large tentacles tear
away easily (octopus will produce sufficient juice for cooking).
Drain octopus and cool. Pull off large tentacles, then peel
away thick skin and cut tentacles into 5cm-long strips
and bodies into wide strips. Toss octopus with remaining
ingredients in a large bowl, season to taste with sea salt
and freshly ground black pepper, then transfer to a plastic
container, cover tightly and refrigerate.

Serve pickled octopus chilled or at room temperature
with olives and ouzo, if using.

Serves 6-8

Greek cooks prefer the
more pungent flavour of dried
oregano (rigani) to fresh varieties.
It is available in stems from
continental delicatessens.

Oregano and paprika stuffed sardines

Olive oil
3 shallots, thinly sliced
1 tablespoon oregano leaves
20g (½ cup) breadcrumbs, made from day-old bread
Finely grated rind of 1 lemon
1 teaspoon sweet smoked Spanish paprika
18 small sardines (about 40g each), cleaned
1½ tablespoons lemon juice
Crusty bread and lemon wedges, optional, to serve

Sardines are an oily fish; they are at their most delicious when teamed with other strong flavours.

Heat 2 tablespoons oil in a frying pan, add shallots and cook over low heat for 5-6 minutes or until just soft. Increase heat to medium, then add oregano and breadcrumbs and stir for 5 minutes or until breadcrumbs are golden. Add lemon rind and paprika and season to taste with sea salt and freshly ground black pepper. Cool.

Meanwhile, using a small sharp knife, cut along one side of the backbone of each sardine, making sure not to cut all the way to the belly. Place 1 teaspoon cooled stuffing mixture into each sardine cavity and arrange in a single layer in a lightly oiled ceramic ovenproof dish. Scatter with remaining stuffing mixture, drizzle with lemon juice and 1 tablespoon oil, then bake at 190C for 10 minutes or until just cooked through.

Serve sardines warm or at room temperature with crusty bread and lemon wedges, if using.

Serves 6

Hot-smoking refers to a curing process by which the fish is partially or totally cooked at extremely low temperatures over a period of some hours.

Trout tapenade

300g whole hot-smoked trout, flesh removed and flaked

180g Sicilian or other large green olives, pitted

1 large clove of garlic, crushed

100ml extra virgin olive oil

Grated rind and juice of 1 lemon

⅓ cup (firmly packed) basil leaves

Wood-fired bread, sliced on the diagonal, drizzled with olive oil and toasted, to serve

Process all ingredients in a food processor until coarsely chopped. Season to taste with sea salt and freshly ground black pepper, transfer to a bowl and serve at room temperature with wood-fired bread.

Trout tapenade will keep, closely covered and refrigerated, for up to 3 days.

Makes about 1¼ cups

Pea and mint pancakes with scallops and leeks

60g butter, plus extra, for cooking
2 small leeks, very thinly sliced
12 large scallops (about 240g), without roe
½ cup pouring cream
Chervil sprigs, optional, to serve

PEA AND MINT PANCAKES
275g shelled peas (about 850g in pod)
1 tablespoon (firmly packed) mint leaves
1 egg
1 egg yolk
⅓ cup pouring cream
35g (¼ cup) plain flour
40g butter, melted and cooled

Melt 40g butter in a frying pan, add leeks and stir frequently over medium heat for 15 minutes or until tender.

Meanwhile, for pea and mint pancakes, cook peas in boiling salted water for 5 minutes or until tender, add mint leaves, drain immediately, then refresh in iced water and drain again. Reserve 50g peas, then process remaining peas and mint in a food processor until smooth. Add egg, egg yolk and cream and process until combined, then add flour and butter, process briefly until just incorporated, and season to taste with sea salt and freshly ground black pepper.

Heat a little extra butter in a non-stick frying pan and cook heaped tablespoonfuls of pancake mixture, in batches, over medium heat for 2 minutes on each side or until lightly golden. Keep pancakes warm in a 150C oven while cooking remaining pancakes.

Heat 10g butter in a heavy-based frying pan, add half the scallops and cook over medium-high heat for 30 seconds on each side, then remove from pan. Repeat with remaining butter and scallops, then season scallops to taste.

Add cream to leek mixture and bring to the boil, then season to taste. Divide three-quarters leek mixture among 4 shallow bowls and top each with 3 pancakes, then remaining leek mixture. Divide scallops and reserved peas among bowls and serve immediately, scattered with chervil, if using.

Serves 4

Prawn, prosciutto and creamed egg roulade

3 eggs

2 egg yolks

20g butter

1 tablespoon double cream

8 slices prosciutto (about 80g)

500g small cooked prawns, peeled and cleaned

Herb salad, optional, to serve

ROULADE

40g butter

35g (¼ cup) plain flour

1 cup milk

3 eggs, separated

Purchase your prosciutto from a delicatessen that will slice to order, to prevent it from drying out.

For roulade, melt butter in a small saucepan, add flour and stir over low heat for 1-2 minutes or until grainy. Whisking continuously, gradually add milk, then cook for another 2 minutes. Remove from heat, cool slightly, then stir in egg yolks, one at a time, beating well after each addition. Season to taste with sea salt, then transfer mixture to a small bowl, cover closely with plastic wrap and cool to room temperature. Using an electric mixer, whisk egg whites until stiff peaks form, then gently fold egg whites into cooled egg mixture. Pour mixture into a baking-paper-lined 23x33cm shallow oven tray, smooth top and bake at 200C for 15-20 minutes or until just set and barely coloured. Turn roulade out onto a clean tea towel, peel off baking paper, then carefully roll up from one long side, and cool, wrapped in tea towel.

Place eggs and egg yolks in a bowl, season to taste with sea salt and freshly ground black pepper and lightly beat. Melt butter in a heavy-based frying pan, add eggs and stir continuously over low heat with a wooden spoon for 6-8 minutes or until eggs are thick and smooth but still slightly runny. Do not overheat. Remove from heat and stir in cream. Carefully unroll roulade, then spread a very thin layer of egg mixture over roulade, leaving a 1cm border. Place prosciutto in a single layer over egg mixture, then spread remaining egg mixture over prosciutto. Place prawns along long side of roulade, then roll up roulade, wrap tightly in plastic wrap, twist ends to seal and refrigerate for 1 hour.

To serve, unwrap roulade, then cut into 2cm-thick slices and serve immediately with a herb salad, if using.

Serves 6

Fried squid with pinenut and parsley tarator

110g (¾ cup) plain flour

1 teaspoon cayenne

Vegetable oil, for deep-frying

750g baby squid, cleaned and cut into
5mm-wide rings

Lime wedges, optional, to serve

PINENUT AND PARSLEY TARATOR

1 clove of garlic, finely chopped

80g (½ cup) pinenuts

35g (½ cup) fresh white breadcrumbs

2 tablespoons lemon juice, or to taste

½ cup olive oil

¼ cup (firmly packed) flat-leaf parsley
leaves, coarsely chopped

For pinenut and parsley tarator, place garlic on a work surface, sprinkle with ½ teaspoon sea salt and, using the back of a large knife, crush garlic until a smooth paste forms. Transfer garlic paste to the bowl of a small food processor, add pinenuts and breadcrumbs and process until finely chopped, then add lemon juice and 2 teaspoons water and process to combine well. Add olive oil in a thin steady stream and process until well combined and emulsified, then transfer tarator to a small bowl, stir in parsley and season to taste with sea salt and freshly ground black pepper. Cover closely with plastic wrap and refrigerate until needed. Makes about ¾ cup.

Combine flour and cayenne in a bowl and season to taste. Fill a large saucepan or deep-fryer one-third full of oil and heat to 200C. Working in batches, dust squid in seasoned flour, shaking off excess, and deep-fry for 1-2 minutes or until crisp and light golden. Drain on absorbent paper, sprinkle with sea salt and serve with pinenut and parsley tarator and lime wedges to the side, if using.

Serves 6

David Tsirekas' crab and dill dolmades with saffron cream avgolemono

David Tsirekas is chef/co-owner of Perama Greek restaurant in Sydney.

24-30 large preserved vine leaves, soaked in water for 1 hour, then drained

40g butter

1 leek, white part only, quartered lengthways and finely chopped

1 small Spanish onion, finely chopped

500g blue swimmer or spanner crab meat, picked through

2 tablespoons mayonnaise

25ml ouzo

¼ cup chopped dill

SAFFRON CREAM AVGOLEMONO

3 egg yolks

Juice of 1 large lemon

1 cup thickened cream

Large pinch of saffron threads

Steam vine leaves, covered, over boiling water for 5 minutes or until just tender, then refresh in iced water, drain well and pat dry with absorbent paper.

Heat butter in a frying pan, add leek and onion and cook over low heat for 8-10 minutes or until very soft. Drain leek mixture in a sieve over a bowl, pressing down lightly with a wooden spoon to extract juices, then reserve juices and cool vegetables to room temperature.

Combine crabmeat and drained leek mixture with remaining ingredients in a large bowl, then season to taste with sea salt and freshly ground black pepper.

Place 1 vine leaf flat on a work surface and place 1 tablespoon crab filling in the centre at the base of leaf. Fold both sides of leaf over filling, then roll up to form a small log-shaped parcel, taking care not to roll too tightly. Repeat with remaining leaves and filling, then, if not serving immediately, refrigerate, covered, until ready to serve.

For saffron cream avgolemono, whisk egg yolks and lemon juice in a bowl until combined. Place cream, saffron threads and reserved leek and onion juices in a small saucepan and slowly bring to the boil over low-medium heat, then remove from heat immediately and cool for 5 minutes. Add 1 tablespoon cream mixture to egg mixture, whisk until well combined and frothy, then transfer to pan with cream mixture. Whisk sauce continuously over low heat for 2 minutes or until mixture thickens enough to coat the back of a spoon, taking care not to boil, then remove from heat.

Serve saffron cream avgolemono immediately, or at room temperature, with crab and dill dolmades. Best made on day of serving.

Serves 6

Of the two varieties of tarragon available, always choose French tarragon over Russian tarragon. The former can be distinguished by its delicate slender leaves, aniseed flavour and subtle aroma; the latter has much coarser leaves and a grassy flavour.

Prawn and fennel fritto misto with tarragon egg sauce

150g (¾ cup) fine semolina

1½ tablespoons dried Greek oregano

Vegetable oil, for deep-frying

3 bulbs of baby fennel, quartered

12 green king prawns, peeled, heads and tails intact

TARRAGON EGG SAUCE

2 hard-boiled eggs, yolks and whites separated, finely chopped

½ cup French tarragon leaves, finely chopped

6 anchovy fillets, chopped

1 tablespoon capers, rinsed and chopped

1 tablespoon red wine vinegar

⅓ cup extra virgin olive oil

For tarragon egg sauce, place all ingredients in a bowl, season to taste with sea salt and freshly ground black pepper and combine well. Makes about 1 cup.

Combine semolina and oregano in a bowl and season to taste.

Heat oil in a large saucepan or deep fryer to 180C. Toss fennel and prawns, in batches, in seasoned semolina, shaking off excess, and deep-fry fennel for 2-3 minutes and prawns for 1 minute or until just cooked. Drain on absorbent paper, season to taste with sea salt and serve immediately with tarragon egg sauce.

Serves 6

Anthony Musarra's pressed swordfish and potato terrine with caper, lemon and olive dressing

This recipe is one of the signature dishes of highly respected Sydney and Melbourne chef Anthony Musarra.

1kg piece of swordfish or tuna, skinned

1 litre fish stock

1 clove of garlic, chopped

1.2kg desiree potatoes, boiled until just tender, drained and peeled

60g salted capers, rinsed and drained

60g large green olives, pitted

60g cornichons

1½ tablespoons lemon juice

75ml extra virgin olive oil

180g mixed salad leaves

DRESSING

100g large green olives, pitted and finely chopped

80g salted capers, rinsed, drained and finely chopped

50g small black olives, pitted

2 tablespoons coarsely chopped flat-leaf parsley

⅔ cup lemon juice

100ml lemon pressed extra virgin olive oil

4 shallots, thinly sliced

Cut swordfish into 1cm-thick slices. Bring fish stock to the boil in a deep frying pan, reduce heat to low, add garlic and fish and cook for 2 minutes or until fish is tender, but still rare in the centre. Remove fish from stock and cool.

Cut potatoes into 1cm-thick slices and trim edges square. Process capers, olives, cornichons, lemon juice and olive oil in a food processor until smooth, then season to taste with freshly ground black pepper. Line an 8x22cm terrine with plastic wrap and brush with olive oil. Place an even layer of potato in bottom of terrine and spread with a layer of olive mixture. Top with an even layer of swordfish, cutting to fit. Repeat process, finishing with a layer of potato. Cover with plastic wrap, weight down with food cans and refrigerate overnight.

For dressing, combine all ingredients in a bowl and season to taste.

Carefully unmould terrine and, using a finely serrated knife, cut into 2cm-thick slices. Toss salad leaves with a little of the dressing. Place salad leaves on plates, top with slices of terrine and remaining dressing.

Serves 10

Fish and lobster salad with tomato-cumin dressing

600g salmon fillet, skinned
and pin-boned

Olive oil

1 cooked lobster (about 750g), shelled
and thinly sliced

3 egg tomatoes, cut into thin wedges

2 red capsicum, grilled until skin
blackens, then cooled, peeled, seeded
and cut into strips

120g (¾ cup) pitted green Spanish
olives, sliced

1 Spanish onion, cut into very
thin wedges

1 bunch of watercress, sprigs removed

TOMATO-CUMIN DRESSING

2 very ripe egg tomatoes, chopped

2 cloves of garlic, finely chopped

1 tablespoon tomato paste

1½ teaspoons cumin seeds, dry
roasted and coarsely ground

1½ teaspoons sweet Spanish paprika

2 tablespoons sherry vinegar

½ cup extra virgin olive oil

Young acidic sherry from the Jerez de
la Frontera region of Spain is used to
make sherry vinegar, which is matured
in oak sherry casks. It is available from
delicatessens and specialty food stores.

For tomato-cumin dressing, process tomatoes, garlic, tomato
paste, cumin, paprika and vinegar in a food processor until well
combined, then, with motor running, add oil in a thin, steady
stream and process until incorporated. Season to taste with sea
salt and freshly ground pepper. Makes about 2 cups.

Brush salmon with oil, season to taste, then barbecue or char-grill
on a hot plate for 3 minutes on each side or until cooked but still
pink in the middle. Cool, then cut into 2.5cm pieces. Combine
salmon pieces with remaining ingredients in a large bowl, drizzle
with a little tomato-cumin dressing and toss gently to coat.

Divide salad among plates and serve immediately, with
remaining dressing passed separately.

Serves 4 as a main course or 8 as an entrée

Burghul (also known as cracked wheat)
is hulled, steamed wheat kernels that
are dried and crushed into various
sized grains. It can be purchased
from health food stores and
Middle Eastern food stores.

Cucumber, raw ocean trout and burghul salad

240g (1½ cups) fine burghul

150ml extra virgin olive oil

⅓ cup lemon juice, or to taste

1 teaspoon ground coriander

½ teaspoon ground cinnamon

500g piece of ocean trout or salmon, skinned, pin-boned
and cut into 1cm pieces

1 telegraph cucumber, seeded and cut into 1cm pieces

4 green onions, finely chopped

1 large clove of garlic, finely chopped

½ cup chopped flat-leaf parsley

⅓ cup chopped coriander

Soak burghul in cold water for 20 minutes, then drain well, squeezing
out excess liquid. Combine burghul with remaining ingredients in
a large bowl, adding more lemon juice if desired, and season to taste
with sea salt and freshly ground black pepper. Divide salad among
bowls and serve immediately.

Serves 6-8 as an entrée or light lunch

Squid and broad bean salad

¼ cup extra virgin olive oil

2 cloves of garlic, finely chopped

3 anchovy fillets, finely chopped

Pinch of dried chilli flakes

2 teaspoons white wine vinegar

1kg fresh broad beans, podded, or 500g packet
frozen broad beans, thawed

200g sugarsnap peas, trimmed

750g cleaned squid tubes, cut into 8mm-thick slices

½ cup (firmly packed) flat-leaf parsley leaves, chopped

2 tablespoons lemon juice

Look for Ortiz Spanish anchovies in olive oil; these are hand-filleted which preserves their delicate texture and taste. They are available from specialty food stores. Alternatively, use other anchovies that have been canned in olive oil.

Combine olive oil, garlic, anchovies and chilli flakes in a small frying pan and cook over low heat for 2-3 minutes or until garlic is light golden, then add vinegar and transfer to a large bowl.

Steam broad beans over a saucepan of simmering water for 3 minutes or until tender. Cool beans slightly, then peel and add to garlic mixture. Steam sugarsnap peas over a saucepan of simmering water for 3 minutes or until tender, then add to beans. Steam squid rings, in batches if necessary, over a saucepan of simmering water for 2-3 minutes or until just tender, then add to bean mixture. Add parsley and lemon juice, season to taste with sea salt and freshly ground black pepper and mix well. Serve warm or at room temperature, divided among shallow bowls.

Serves 6 as a light lunch

Grilled cuttlefish and chickpea salad

1.5kg cuttlefish, cleaned, tentacles reserved and hoods cut open

Extra virgin olive oil

2 cloves of garlic, finely chopped

2 Spanish onions, cut into 5mm-wide rings

6 dried small red chillies

1½ teaspoons sweet smoked Spanish paprika

2 teaspoons dried oregano

¼ teaspoon saffron threads

¼ teaspoon cayenne

1 cup freshly squeezed orange juice

1 tablespoon lemon juice

400g can chickpeas, rinsed and drained

1 bunch of coriander, leaves picked and chopped

The flavour and colour derived from saffron threads, the dried stigmas of the purple crocus flower, can vary wildly. The best saffron threads, however, are thought to originate from Spain, and are available from specialty food stores and delicatessens.

Brush cuttlefish tentacles and hoods with olive oil, then char-grill or barbecue over high heat for 40 seconds on each side or until just opaque (large tentacles will take slightly longer to cook). Cool cuttlefish, then cut hoods into thick slices and place in a large bowl with tentacles.

Heat ¼ cup olive oil in a saucepan, add garlic, onions and whole dried chillies and stir over medium heat for 3 minutes or until onions are just soft. Add paprika, oregano, saffron and cayenne, stir for 2 minutes, then add orange and lemon juices and bring to the boil. Remove from heat and cool slightly. Pour mixture over cuttlefish, add chickpeas, then season to taste with sea salt and freshly ground black pepper and combine well. Cool to room temperature, stir in chopped coriander, then divide salad among bowls and serve.

Serves 6 as a light lunch

Tuna, prosciutto and potato salad with raisin and vincotto dressing

Vincotto is made by cooking freshly crushed grapes until syrupy. It has a deep, raisin flavour balanced with a little acidity, and is available from specialty food stores.

4 tuna or swordfish steaks (each about 200g and 1.5cm thick)

Olive oil

600g kipfler potatoes, scrubbed, cooked in boiling salted water and cooled

200g prosciutto, thinly sliced widthways

1 bunch of rocket, trimmed, washed and dried

1 head of radicchio, outer leaves discarded, inner leaves torn into large pieces

DRESSING

1 egg yolk

1½ tablespoons Dijon mustard

1½ tablespoons vincotto

1½ cups olive oil

40g raisins, soaked in boiling water for ½ hour

For dressing, combine egg yolk, mustard and vincotto in a large bowl and whisk to combine well. Whisking continuously, add olive oil, drop by drop at first, then in a slow, steady stream until mixture is emulsified and thick. Drain raisins, reserving soaking liquid, stir raisins into dressing, then add enough soaking liquid to thin to a pouring consistency. Season to taste with sea salt and freshly ground black pepper, then cover and set aside at room temperature.

Brush tuna with olive oil. Heat a heavy-based frying pan until very hot, add 2 tuna steaks and cook 1-1½ minutes on each side for medium-rare or until cooked to your liking. Repeat with remaining tuna steaks, then thinly slice tuna. Halve potatoes lengthways, then toss with tuna, prosciutto, rocket and radicchio in a bowl to combine well. Divide salad among plates, drizzle with dressing to taste, and serve immediately.

Serves 4 as a main course or 6 as an entrée

Balmain or Moreton Bay bugs are medium-sized crustaceans with sweet, rich, white flesh. If bugs are unavailable, crayfish or prawns make good substitutes.

Middle Eastern salad with bugs and yoghurt-tahini sauce

2 rounds Lebanese bread, split in half

6 red radishes, trimmed, washed, halved and thinly sliced

1 Lebanese cucumber, peeled, quartered lengthways and cut into 1cm pieces

4 vine-ripened tomatoes (about 650g), each cut into 8 wedges, then cut in half

2 green onions, finely chopped

½ cup coarsely chopped coriander

2 cups coarsely chopped flat-leaf parsley

¼ cup extra virgin olive oil

1½ tablespoons aged white wine vinegar

12 cooked Balmain or Moreton Bay bugs, peeled, halved lengthways and cleaned

1 teaspoon sumac

YOGHURT-TAHINI SAUCE

1 cup Greek-style yoghurt

2 tablespoons tahini

1 clove of garlic, bruised

¼ teaspoon ground cumin

1 tablespoon lemon juice

For yoghurt-tahini sauce, place all ingredients, ½ teaspoon sea salt, pinch of caster sugar and ¼ cup water in a small bowl and stir until smooth and well combined, then cover and refrigerate until needed. Just before serving, discard garlic.

Place bread on an oven tray and bake at 190C for 5-8 minutes or until light golden and crisp, then cool.

Place vegetables and herbs in a large bowl, drizzle with olive oil and vinegar, then break bread into small pieces over bowl and toss gently to combine. To serve, divide salad among 4 bowls, then top with bugs. Drizzle with yoghurt-tahini sauce, sprinkle with a little sumac and serve immediately.

Serves 4 as an entrée or light lunch

Kaffir lime, king prawn and green mango salad

5 kaffir lime leaves, centre vein removed, cut into julienne

¼ cup lime juice

Finely grated rind of 1 lime

⅓ cup vegetable oil

2 fresh red birdseye chillies, seeded and finely chopped

2 large cloves of garlic, finely chopped

2 teaspoons fish sauce

¼ cup Thai basil leaves, chopped, plus extra, to serve

1kg green king prawns, peeled and cleaned, leaving tails intact

Lime wedges, optional, and coriander leaves, to serve

GREEN MANGO SALAD

2 green mangoes, peeled and coarsely grated

1 fresh red birdseye chilli, thinly sliced

2 red shallots, finely chopped

1 tablespoon fish sauce

2 teaspoons lime juice

2 teaspoons rice vinegar

2 teaspoons caster sugar

1 tablespoon chopped Thai basil

1 tablespoon chopped coriander

For green mango salad, combine mango, chilli and shallots in a bowl, then cover and refrigerate until required. Place fish sauce, lime juice, rice vinegar and sugar in a small bowl and stir until sugar dissolves. Just before serving, pour dressing over salad, add basil and coriander and toss to combine well.

Combine kaffir lime leaves, lime juice and rind, oil, chillies, garlic, fish sauce and basil in a small bowl. Place prawns in a ceramic or glass bowl, pour marinade over and toss to coat well, then cover and refrigerate for 10 minutes.

Barbecue or char-grill prawns for 1-2 minutes on each side or until cooked through. Serve immediately with green mango salad, lime wedges, if using, coriander leaves and extra Thai basil leaves.

Serves 4 as an entrée or light lunch

Thai basil (also known as bai horapha) has smaller leaves than common (sweet) basil, purple stems and a slight anise taste.

Chervil has a mild aniseed flavour and small, fern-like leaves. When combined in equal quantities with chives, parsley and tarragon, it becomes the classic French herb mixture, fines herbes.

Prawn, scallop, fennel and chervil salad

½ carrot, finely chopped

½ onion, finely chopped

1 stalk of celery, finely chopped

1 tablespoon white wine vinegar

2 dried bay leaves

1kg medium green prawns, heads removed, cleaned

2 bulbs of baby fennel (about 600g), thinly sliced

Juice and thinly peeled rind of 1 lemon, rind cut into julienne

600g scallops, without roe

Extra virgin olive oil

½ cup chervil sprigs, coarsely chopped

Place carrot, onion, celery, vinegar and bay leaves in a large saucepan, fill with water and bring to the boil. Add prawns and return to the boil, then cook until shells turn red. Drain immediately, discarding liquid and vegetables. Cool slightly, then peel prawns and transfer to a large bowl.

Combine fennel, lemon juice and rind in a large bowl, then add to prawns.

Brush scallops lightly with olive oil, then char-grill or barbecue for 45 seconds on each side or until just cooked, season to taste with sea salt and freshly ground black pepper, then add to prawns. Add ¼ cup olive oil and chervil, season to taste and toss gently to combine. Serve salad immediately.

Serves 4 as a main course or 6 as an entrée

Salad of linguine, sardines, eggplant, basil and breadcrumbs

85g (1¼ cups) coarse fresh breadcrumbs

Extra virgin olive oil

700g sardine fillets

2 onions, halved and thinly sliced

600g small Lebanese eggplant (about 10), sliced lengthways

350g dried linguine, cooked in boiling salted water until al dente, then refreshed, drained and tossed with 1 tablespoon olive oil

160g (1 cup) dried black olives, pitted

½ cup basil leaves, torn if large

¼ cup balsamic or red wine vinegar, or to taste

Dried black olives are characterised by a very concentrated, salty flavour, and are available from continental delicatessens.

Toss breadcrumbs in just enough olive oil to coat, spread in a thin layer on an oven tray and cook at 180C, stirring often, for 15 minutes or until golden. Cool.

Brush sardine fillets with olive oil, then char-grill, skin-side down, over medium-high heat for 3 minutes or until nearly cooked through, turn over and cook for 30 seconds, then remove from heat. Halve or break up sardines. Brush onions and eggplant with oil, then char-grill, in batches, over medium heat for 2 minutes on each side or until lightly charred and soft. Gently toss sardines, onions and eggplant with breadcrumbs and remaining ingredients until just combined, then divide among 6 bowls and serve immediately.

Serves 6 as a main course

Crumbed garfish, ruby grapefruit and avocado salad with chive vinaigrette

4 garfish, butterflied

Plain flour, seasoned to taste, for dusting

2 eggs, lightly beaten with
1 tablespoon milk

140g (2 cups) breadcrumbs, made
from day-old bread

Finely grated rind of 1 lemon

Olive oil

2 heads of baby cos, leaves separated
and cut into 4cm-wide slices

2 ruby grapefruit, peeled and
segmented, 1 tablespoon juice
reserved for chive vinaigrette

2 avocados, halved, seeded, peeled
and cut into chunks

CHIVE VINAIGRETTE

2 teaspoons Dijon mustard

2 teaspoons sherry vinegar

⅓ cup extra virgin olive oil

¼ cup finely chopped chives
(about 1 bunch)

Sand whiting or King George whiting,
also delicate-fleshed fish, may be
substituted for the garfish in this
recipe. Scallops, too, would work
well with the flavours of this dish.

For chive vinaigrette, combine mustard, vinegar and reserved
grapefruit juice in a small bowl and gradually whisk in olive oil until
well combined and emulsified. Season to taste with sea salt and
freshly ground black pepper and stir in chives just before serving.

Dust garfish in seasoned flour, shaking off excess, then dip in
beaten egg mixture, then in combined breadcrumbs and lemon rind,
pressing firmly to coat. Heat just enough olive oil to cover the base
of a heavy-based frying and cook crumbed garfish, in batches, over
medium heat for 2 minutes on each side or until golden and just
cooked through, then drain on absorbent paper.

Combine cos lettuce, grapefruit segments, avocado and chive
vinaigrette in a bowl and toss gently to combine, then divide among
4 plates, top with garfish and serve immediately.

Serves 4 as a light lunch

Swordfish and artichoke salad niçoise

350g baby green beans, topped

3 swordfish or tuna steaks (each about 300g and 2.5cm thick)

Olive oil

250g truss cherry tomatoes, separated

1 butter lettuce, trimmed, leaves separated, washed and dried

150g drained quartered preserved artichoke hearts in olive oil

1 tablespoon small capers

60g small black olives

3 hard-boiled eggs, shelled and quartered

3 anchovy fillets, halved lengthways

DRESSING

100ml olive oil

½ clove of garlic, finely chopped

¼ cup (firmly packed) basil leaves

1½ tablespoons aged white wine vinegar

For dressing, process olive oil, garlic and basil in a small food processor until very finely chopped, then, just before serving, whisk in white wine vinegar and season to taste with sea salt and freshly ground black pepper.

Cook green beans in boiling salted water until almost tender, drain and refresh in iced water, then drain again.

Brush swordfish steaks lightly with olive oil. Heat a heavy-based frying pan until very hot, and cook steaks, in batches, for 1½ minutes on each side for medium rare or until cooked to your liking. Remove swordfish from pan and cool slightly. Add tomatoes to same pan, cover with a lid and cook for 2-3 minutes, shaking pan occasionally or until tomatoes are just soft and skins have burst.

Toss green beans with 2 tablespoons dressing. Divide lettuce leaves among plates, then top with green beans, cooked tomatoes, preserved artichokes, capers, olives and egg. Break swordfish into 3-4cm pieces and place over salad with anchovies. Drizzle with remaining dressing and serve immediately.

Serves 4 as a main course or 6 as a light lunch

Seafood paella with alioli

500g medium green prawns

500g black mussels, scrubbed
and bearded

2 cups hot fish or chicken stock

¼ cup olive oil

1 onion, finely chopped

3 cloves of garlic, finely chopped

5 tomatoes (about 850g), peeled,
seeded and finely chopped

½ teaspoon saffron threads,
soaked in 2 tablespoons boiling
water for 10 minutes

300g (1½ cups) Calasparra or
arborio rice

250g green lobster tail, halved
lengthways then widthways

350g small squid, cleaned
and cut into rings

ALIOLI

3 cloves of garlic, chopped

2 egg yolks

2 tablespoons lemon juice

200ml olive oil

Peel and clean prawns, leaving tails intact and reserving heads and shells. Place prawn heads and shells in a saucepan, cover with 3 cups water and simmer over medium heat for 20 minutes, then strain into another saucepan and discard solids. Bring liquid to the boil and reduce to 1 cup.

Place mussels and 1 tablespoon water in a saucepan and cook, covered, over medium heat for 4-5 minutes or until opened. Remove mussels, discard any unopened ones, reserve mussel liquid and remove meatless shell from each mussel. Add strained reserved mussel liquid and fish or chicken stock to prawn stock and season to taste with sea salt and freshly ground black pepper.

Heat oil in a 34cm paella pan or frying pan and cook onion over low heat until soft. Add garlic, tomatoes and saffron mixture and cook over high heat until tomatoes are very thick and pulpy. Add rice and stir to coat with mixture. Add 1 cup of stock mixture and cook over high heat for 5 minutes, moving pan to distribute heat and to create a crust on base of pan. Add three-quarters of remaining stock mixture, prawns, lobster and squid. Do not stir again. Cook over medium heat for another 10 minutes, then add mussels. Cook for another 5 minutes or until seafood is cooked, rice is tender, liquid has been absorbed and mixture is quite dry, adding more stock mixture if necessary. Remove from heat, cover with a clean tea towel and stand for 10 minutes before serving with alioli.

For alioli, process garlic, egg yolks and lemon juice in a food processor until smooth. With motor running, gradually add olive oil in a thin, steady stream until thick, then season to taste. Thin with a little warm water, if necessary, to achieve desired consistency. Makes about 1½ cups.

Serves 4

Lobster with lemon, orzo and caperberries

2 green lobster tails (about 250g each)
400g orzo (risoni)
¼ cup extra virgin olive oil
1 clove of garlic, finely chopped
2 shallots, finely chopped
375ml dry white wine
120g cold unsalted butter, chopped
Rind of 1 lemon, cut into julienne
1 tablespoon chopped caperberries
¼ cup flat-leaf parsley, chopped

Place lobster tails, shell-side down, on a work surface and, using a heavy kitchen knife, cut each into 6 widthways.

Cook orzo in plenty of boiling salted water for 10 minutes or until al dente. Drain and toss with 1 tablespoon olive oil, then season to taste with sea salt and freshly ground black pepper.

Heat remaining olive oil in a large frying pan, add garlic and shallots and stir over low heat until fragrant. Add lobster pieces and cook for 4 minutes, turn and cook for another 3-4 minutes or until flesh is opaque. Remove lobster from pan and keep warm. Add white wine to pan, stir well and bring to the boil, then simmer for 2-3 minutes or until slightly reduced. Gradually whisk in butter over low heat until all the butter is incorporated. Add lemon rind and chopped caperberries, then adjust seasoning to taste and stir in parsley until well combined. Divide orzo among warm plates, top with lobster pieces and pour sauce over.

Serves 6

If green lobster tails prove difficult to source, they can be substituted with green Balmain or Moreton Bay bugs or even large green prawns.

Clams should be soaked in cold
fresh water for at least 2-3 hours
prior to use – time enough for
these bivalve molluscs
to expel any sand.

Spaghetti with clams, saffron and leek

20g butter

1 tablespoon olive oil

1 large leek, washed well and thinly sliced

4 cloves of garlic, crushed

125ml dry white wine

½ cup chicken stock

1 cup pouring cream

Large pinch of saffron threads, soaked in 1 tablespoon
boiling water for 10 minutes

1kg clams (vongole), soaked in cold water

400g spaghetti

2 teaspoons chopped dill

1 tablespoon chopped flat-leaf parsley

2 tablespoons lemon juice

Heat butter and oil in a large saucepan, add leek and garlic and
cook, stirring occasionally, over low heat for 10 minutes or until soft.
Add wine, increase heat to medium and simmer until reduced by
half. Add chicken stock, cream and saffron mixture and simmer
for 10 minutes or until the sauce begins to thicken. Add clams,
cover and cook for 5-8 minutes or until clams open. Discard any
unopened clams.

Meanwhile, cook spaghetti in plenty of boiling salted water until
al dente, then drain well.

Stir dill, parsley and lemon juice into clam mixture, season to taste
with sea salt and freshly ground black pepper, add spaghetti
and toss gently to combine. Serve immediately.

Serves 4

Prawn, rocket and anchovy orecchiette with chilli pangrattato

500g orecchiette

Extra virgin olive oil

4 cloves of garlic, finely chopped

16 anchovy fillets, chopped

2 tablespoons salted capers,
rinsed well and drained

1kg medium green prawns, peeled,
cleaned and halved lengthways

2 bunches of rocket (about 220g),
coarsely chopped

1 cup (firmly packed) mint,
coarsely chopped

Finely grated rind of 1 lemon

Juice of ½ lemon, or to taste

CHILLI PANGRATTATO

1 teaspoon dried chilli flakes

¼ cup extra virgin olive oil

⅓ loaf day-old ciabatta (about 165g),
crust removed, bread torn into
bite-size pieces

For chilli pangrattato, place chilli flakes and oil in a small saucepan and cook over low heat for 1-2 minutes or until just warm. Remove from heat, cool, then strain oil into a small bowl and discard chilli flakes. Place torn bread on an oven tray, drizzle with chilli oil, season to taste with sea salt and freshly ground black pepper and toss to combine well, then bake at 180C for 15 minutes or until golden and crisp.

Cook pasta in boiling salted water until al dente, then drain.

Meanwhile, heat ⅓ cup olive oil in a heavy-based frying pan and cook garlic over low heat for 2 minutes or until fragrant. Add anchovies and capers and stir for another 2 minutes, then increase heat to high, add prawns and stir for 3-4 minutes or until prawns just change colour. Add drained pasta, rocket, mint, lemon rind and juice and season to taste, then stir over low heat until rocket is just wilted. Divide prawn, rocket and anchovy orecchiette among warm bowls, scatter with chilli pangrattato and drizzle with a little extra olive oil if desired, then serve immediately.

Serves 4

As a substitute for orecchiette
(small ear-shaped pasta), use
other dried short pasta such as
farfalle, strozzapreti or spirali.

Mussel, cauliflower and caper ravioli with green olive dressing

1kg black mussels, scrubbed and bearded

Extra virgin olive oil

4 cloves of garlic, finely chopped

1½ tablespoons capers, rinsed
and drained

¼ small head of cauliflower (about 300g),
trimmed and cut into florets

⅓ cup verjuice

8 anchovy fillets, chopped

50g (⅓ cup) pinenuts, roasted

⅓ cup coarsely chopped flat-leaf parsley

250g packet of egg wonton wrappers

GREEN OLIVE DRESSING

¼ cup thyme leaves

200g Sicilian green olives (available from
Italian delicatessens) or other large green
olives, flesh removed in wide slices

½ cup extra virgin olive oil

1 tablespoon lemon juice, or to taste

Bring ¼ cup water to the boil in a heavy-based frying pan, then cook mussels, in batches, covered over high heat for 2-3 minutes or until just opened. Transfer cooked mussels to a colander placed over a bowl, then, when cool enough to handle, remove meat from shells, discarding any unopened mussels, then coarsely chop mussel meat.

Heat ¼ cup olive oil in a heavy-based frying pan, add garlic and capers and cook over low heat for 3-4 minutes or until garlic is just beginning to brown. Add cauliflower and verjuice, combine well, then cook, covered for 10-12 minutes or until cauliflower is very tender. Add anchovies, increase heat to medium and cook, uncovered for 4-5 minutes or until most of the liquid has evaporated, then stir in mussels and pinenuts and season to taste with sea salt and freshly ground black pepper. Cool, then stir in parsley.

For green olive dressing, combine all ingredients in a bowl, season to taste and stand at room temperature until ready to serve.

Working with 2 wrappers at a time, place 2 teaspoons mussel filling in the centre of one wrapper, lightly brush outer edges with water, place another wrapper on top, pressing edges firmly to seal, then place on a tea towel-lined tray.

Cook ravioli in gently simmering salted water for 3-4 minutes or until just tender, drain well, then divide among warm shallow bowls, drizzle with green olive dressing and serve immediately.

Serves 6

Prawn, feta and dill pilaf

Feta was originally made by nomadic shepherds in the Eastern Mediterranean from a combination of goat's and sheep's milk. Today, it is made from cow's, sheep's or goat's milk; the latter two varieties are considered superior.

2½ tablespoons extra virgin olive oil

1 onion, finely chopped

2 cloves of garlic, finely chopped

2 dried bay leaves

¾ teaspoon ground allspice

50g (⅓ cup) currants

400g (2 cups) basmati rice, washed, soaked for 30 minutes, then drained

800ml chicken stock

1kg small green king prawns, peeled and cleaned

175g feta, coarsely crumbled

¼ cup coarsely chopped flat-leaf parsley

2 tablespoons chopped dill

Heat oil in a large, heavy-based saucepan, add onion, garlic and bay leaves and stir over medium heat for 5 minutes or until onion is soft, then add allspice, currants and rice and stir to combine well. Add stock, bring mixture to the boil, cover with a tight-fitting lid and reduce heat to very low, then cook for 12 minutes or until rice is nearly cooked. Add prawns, stirring gently to combine with rice mixture, and cook, covered for another 3 minutes, then remove pilaf from heat and stand, covered for 5 minutes or until prawns are just cooked. Gently stir in feta and herbs, season pilaf to taste with sea salt and freshly ground black pepper and serve immediately.

Serves 6

The colour of a mango is not indicative of its ripeness; varieties range from green, to those with a red blush, to orange. The best indicator of ripeness is smell; a ripe mango will have a sweet perfume.

Tequila prawns with mango salsa and soft tortillas

1 tablespoon caster sugar

1 tablespoon white wine vinegar

¾ cup strained mandarin juice (about 3 mandarins)

Olive oil

1 fresh red birdseye chilli, seeded and finely chopped

2 tablespoons tequila

¼ cup mint leaves, finely shredded

16 extra-large green king prawns (about 1.5kg), or giant green freshwater prawns, peeled and cleaned with tails intact

8 thick bamboo skewers, soaked in water for 30 minutes

4 limes, halved

16 soft flour tortillas, wrapped in foil and warmed in a hot oven

MANGO SALSA

2 tablespoons lime juice

½ fresh red birdseye chilli, seeded and finely chopped

2 mangoes, peeled, stoned and finely chopped

Place sugar, vinegar, juice, ¼ cup olive oil, chilli, tequila and mint in a bowl and mix well.

Thread 2 prawns onto each bamboo skewer and place in a shallow glass or ceramic dish. Reserve 2 tablespoons marinade, then drizzle remaining marinade over prawns and turn to coat. Cover and refrigerate for 10 minutes for flavours to develop.

Meanwhile, for mango salsa, combine reserved marinade, lime juice, chilli and mango, season to taste with sea salt and mix well.

Drain prawns from marinade and barbecue or char-grill on an oiled char-grill pan, in batches, for 2-3 minutes on each side or until just cooked. Barbecue or char-grill lime halves, cut-side down, until golden.

Serve prawn skewers and lime halves immediately with mango salsa and warm tortillas.

Serves 4

If you prefer, dry white wine can be substituted for the dry cider (fermented apple juice) in this recipe.

Mussel and clam gratins

125ml dry cider

2 sprigs of thyme

2kg black mussels, scrubbed and bearded

1.8kg clams (vongole), soaked in cold water

35g (½ cup) breadcrumbs, made from day-old bread

Finely grated rind of 1 lemon

½ cup flat-leaf parsley, finely chopped

½ cup dill sprigs, chopped

100g butter, chopped

4 cloves of garlic, finely chopped

Place cider and thyme in a wide heavy-based saucepan and bring to the boil. Working in batches, cook mussels and clams in cider, in a single layer, covered, for 1-2 minutes or until just opened. Transfer to a colander placed over a bowl, discarding any unopened shellfish, then strain liquid through a fine sieve and reserve.

Remove mussel meat from shells, then divide clams among 6 shallow ½-cup-capacity heatproof dishes and scatter with mussel meat. Pour 1½ tablespoons reserved cooking liquid over each dish, then place on an oven tray. Combine breadcrumbs, lemon rind and herbs in a bowl and season to taste with sea salt and freshly ground black pepper.

Melt butter in a small frying pan, add garlic and stir over low heat for 3 minutes or until fragrant but not browned. Drizzle 1 tablespoon garlic mixture over each dish, then return pan to heat, add breadcrumb mixture to remaining butter in pan and stir over low heat for 2 minutes or until well combined. Sprinkle breadcrumb mixture evenly over shellfish, then place under a hot grill for 2-3 minutes or until breadcrumbs are golden and crisp. Serve immediately.

Serves 6

Although pizza dough is easy to make, if you're short on time you can usually purchase pizza dough from your local pizzeria.

Octopus, wild oregano and chilli pizza

⅓ cup extra virgin olive oil

3 cloves of garlic, finely chopped

1 fresh long red chilli, seeded and finely chopped

3 teaspoons dried Greek oregano

750g baby octopus, cleaned

120g (¾ cup) Kalamata olives, pitted

250g grape or cherry tomatoes, halved

¼ cup torn flat-leaf parsley leaves

PIZZA BASE

7g sachet of dried yeast

1 teaspoon caster sugar

375g (2½ cups) plain flour

2 tablespoons olive oil

For pizza base, combine yeast, sugar and 300ml lukewarm water in a bowl and stand in a warm place for 10 minutes or until foamy. Place flour in the bowl of an electric mixer fitted with a dough hook, add yeast mixture and olive oil and combine until mixture comes together. Knead dough for another 8 minutes or until smooth and elastic, then transfer to a lightly oiled bowl, turn to coat, cover and stand in a warm draught-free place for 1 hour or until doubled in size.

Meanwhile, combine oil, garlic, chilli and oregano in a large bowl and season to taste with sea salt and freshly ground black pepper. Reserve 2 tablespoons oil mixture, then add octopus, olives and tomatoes to oil mixture in bowl, toss to combine well, cover and refrigerate until needed.

Place 2 heavy-based oven trays in a 230C oven. Knock down dough and divide in half, then roll out each half on a lightly floured surface to make two 30cm rounds and place each round on a piece of baking paper. Brush bases with reserved oil mixture, leaving a 1cm border, then scatter bases evenly with octopus mixture. Using the baking paper as a support, transfer pizzas to preheated oven trays and bake for 20 minutes, swapping trays during cooking, or until bases are crisp and golden. Scatter with parsley, cut into wedges and serve immediately.

Makes 2 pizzas (each serves 2)

Grilled red mullet with spinach rice and spring herb latholemono

Olive oil

1 large onion, finely chopped

300g (1½ cups) long grain rice

Finely grated rind of 1 lemon

2 bunches of dill

75g (about 3 cups) baby spinach leaves, stalks trimmed

8 red mullet fillets (about 80g each), pin-boned

LATHOLEMONO

½ cup extra virgin olive oil

¼ cup lemon juice

1 tablespoon salted capers, rinsed well, drained and coarsely chopped

1 tablespoon each torn oregano leaves, mint leaves and flat-leaf parsley leaves

2 green onions, thinly sliced

For latholemono, combine all ingredients in a bowl and season to taste with sea salt and freshly ground black pepper, then set aside.

Heat 2 tablespoons olive oil in a heavy-based saucepan, add onion and 1 teaspoon salt and cook, stirring frequently, for 5 minutes or until soft, then add rice and lemon rind and stir for 2 minutes or until lightly toasted. Add 2¼ cups water and bring to the boil, then cook, covered, over low heat for 18-20 minutes or until most of the liquid has been absorbed. Pick 2 tablespoons dill leaves, reserving remaining dill, then add to rice with spinach and season to taste. Remove pan from heat, cover and stand for 5 minutes.

Meanwhile, brush red mullet with a little olive oil, then place remaining dill sprigs on a char-grill or barbecue and place fish on top, flesh-side down, cover loosely with an oiled piece of foil and cook, without turning, for 6-8 minutes or until fish is just tender. Season fish to taste and serve immediately on a bed of spinach rice drizzled with a little latholemono.

Serves 4-6

Charred garfish with fennel and celery salad with walnut and verjuice vinaigrette

60g walnuts, coarsely chopped

½ teaspoon cumin seeds, lightly crushed

1 teaspoon Dijon mustard

¼ cup verjuice

1 teaspoon white wine vinegar

1 tablespoon walnut oil

Olive oil

2 green onions, trimmed to 12cm and thinly sliced on the diagonal

8 garfish, butterflied

FENNEL AND CELERY SALAD

600g fennel (about 2 small bulbs), trimmed, halved lengthways and thinly sliced

3 stalks of celery, trimmed and thinly sliced on the diagonal

1 Spanish onion, halved and thinly sliced

¾ cup coriander leaves

¼ cup extra virgin olive oil

¼ cup red wine vinegar, or to taste

For fennel and celery salad, combine fennel, celery, onion and coriander in a large bowl. Whisk together olive oil and red wine vinegar in small bowl, season to taste with sea salt and freshly ground black pepper, then add to salad and toss gently to combine.

Dry-fry walnuts and cumin seeds in a frying pan until lightly roasted, then cool. Place mustard in a small bowl, gradually whisk in verjuice and vinegar until well combined, then whisk in walnut oil and 1 tablespoon olive oil. Add walnut mixture and green onions and season to taste.

Brush garfish lightly with a little olive oil and season to taste, then char-grill or barbecue, skin-side down, for 1 minute, then turn and cook for another 30-60 seconds or until just cooked through. Place fennel and celery salad onto plates, top with garfish and drizzle generously with walnut and verjuice vinaigrette.

Serves 4

Scallops with shallot and sherry vinegar sauce and sweet potato

Olive oil

4 shallots, finely chopped

Pinch of sweet smoked Spanish paprika

⅓ cup sherry vinegar

2 long, thin orange sweet potatoes (about 750g),
peeled and cut into 1cm-thick slices

10g butter

24 large scallops, without roe

1 tablespoon coarsely chopped flat-leaf parsley

If you prefer, choose scallops with
their edible orange roe still attached.
To prepare scallops, use a small
knife to remove the small opaque
muscle found on the side, as this
can toughen on cooking.

Heat ¼ cup olive oil in a small frying pan, add shallots
and paprika and stir frequently over low heat for 10-15 minutes
or until caramelised. Add sherry vinegar and cook for
2-3 minutes. Remove from heat and season to taste with
sea salt and freshly ground black pepper.

Steam sweet potatoes, covered, in a steamer over boiling
water for 8-10 minutes or until tender, transfer to a bowl,
add one-quarter of the vinegar mixture and mix well.

Heat 1 tablespoon olive oil in a frying pan, add half the butter
and cook half the scallops over high heat for 30-60 seconds on
each side or until just tender. Repeat with another tablespoon
of oil, remaining butter and scallops, then transfer scallops to a
bowl. Add remaining vinegar mixture to the same pan and stir
over medium heat until mixture comes to the boil, then pour
over scallops. Add parsley and toss to combine. Spoon a little
sweet potato mixture into the centre of 4 plates, then spoon
scallop mixture over. Serve warm or at room temperature.

Serves 4

Leek and fish pie

½ cup extra virgin olive oil

2 cloves of garlic, finely chopped

3 leeks (about 600g), trimmed, washed and thinly sliced

85g (½ cup) raisins

75g (½ cup) pitted green olives, coarsely chopped

45g (¼ cup) small salted capers, soaked in water for 1 hour, then rinsed and drained

1 tablespoon finely grated lemon rind

⅓ cup coarsely chopped flat-leaf parsley

600g blue-eye trevalla or other firm-fleshed white fish fillets, cut into 8mm-thick slices

DOUGH

½ teaspoon caster sugar

7g sachet of dried yeast

¼ cup extra virgin olive oil

450g (3 cups) plain flour, approximately

Only the thick, white section of each leek should be used in this recipe; reserve the green tops for use in stock-making.

For dough, combine sugar and ¼ cup lukewarm water in a small bowl, sprinkle with yeast and stand for 10 minutes or until foamy. Transfer yeast mixture to a large bowl, add olive oil and 1 cup lukewarm water, then add 1 teaspoon salt and flour, 1 cup at a time, until a soft dough forms. Knead dough on a floured surface for 5 minutes or until smooth and elastic, shape into a ball, then transfer to a large oiled bowl and turn to coat. Cover bowl with plastic wrap and stand in a warm draught-free place for 1 hour or until doubled in size.

Meanwhile, heat 2 tablespoons olive oil in a large saucepan, add garlic, leeks, raisins, olives and capers and stir over medium heat for 5 minutes or until leeks are soft. Season to taste with sea salt and freshly ground black pepper, then stir in lemon rind and parsley and cool.

Heat ¼ cup olive oil in a large heavy-based frying pan and cook fish, in batches, over high heat for 1 minute on each side. Cool, then combine fish and leek mixture (fish will break up slightly).

Knock down dough, then divide into 4 pieces. Roll out one piece of dough on a lightly floured surface to a 28cm round, then place dough on an oiled 29cm round pizza tray. Scatter half filling mixture over dough, roll a second piece of dough out to form a 28cm round, place over filling, then pinch edges together to seal. Using a knife, make small slits in top of dough and drizzle with a little olive oil. On a second oiled 29cm pizza tray, repeat process with remaining dough, filling and oil. Bake at 200C for 35 minutes or until pies are golden. Cool slightly, cut into wedges and serve.

Serves 6-8

Pancetta-wrapped prawns with borlotti beans and radicchio

3 cloves of garlic, finely chopped

⅔ cup extra virgin olive oil

24 large green king prawns (about 1.5kg), peeled and cleaned, with tails intact

24 bamboo skewers, soaked in water for 30 minutes

24 slices pancetta (about 225g)

BORLOTTI BEANS AND RADICCHIO

2 tablespoons olive oil

2 onions, thinly sliced

2 cloves of garlic, thinly sliced

5 anchovy fillets, chopped

400g (2 cups) dried borlotti beans, soaked in water overnight and drained

2 sprigs of rosemary

1 litre chicken stock

1 head of radicchio, leaves washed, dried and torn into large pieces

Combine garlic, olive oil and 1 teaspoon freshly ground black pepper in a large bowl, add prawns, toss to coat, then cover tightly with plastic wrap and refrigerate for 2 hours.

For borlotti beans and radicchio, heat olive oil in a large saucepan, add onions and garlic and stir over medium heat for 5 minutes or until starting to soften. Add remaining ingredients except radicchio and bring to a simmer, then reduce heat to low and cook for 40 minutes or until beans are soft. Season to taste with sea salt and freshly ground black pepper, then, just before serving, remove rosemary and stir in radicchio while still warm.

Thread each prawn onto a skewer, from head end to tail, then wrap each prawn in a slice of pancetta. Brush skewered prawns with marinating oil, then cook, in batches, on a char-grill plate for 2 minutes on each side or until just cooked. Spoon borlotti beans and radicchio onto plates and top with pancetta-wrapped prawns.

Serves 6

Unlike most salad leaves, the bitter, red-leafed Italian chicory known as radicchio can be used in cooking. The two varieties most widely available, the round-headed chioggia, and treviso, with its elongated leaves, can be used interchangeably.

Stuffed squid baked with potatoes and onion

1.5kg medium squid (about 15cm long), cleaned, tentacles and wings reserved

Extra virgin olive oil

1 onion, finely chopped

2 cloves of garlic, finely chopped

40g (¼ cup) raisins, chopped

120g (1¾ cups) fresh breadcrumbs

60g (¾ cup) grated pecorino

1 teaspoon dried oregano

¼ cup chopped flat-leaf parsley

Large pinch of dried chilli flakes

1 egg, lightly beaten

600g kipfler potatoes, scrubbed and halved lengthways

500g Spanish onions (about 3), cut into wedges

125ml dry white wine

Lemon wedges, to serve

Finely chop squid wings and place in a large bowl. Heat 2½ tablespoons olive oil in a saucepan, add onion, garlic and raisins and stir over medium heat for 5 minutes or until soft, then cool slightly. Add onion mixture, breadcrumbs, pecorino, herbs, chilli flakes and egg to chopped squid wings, then season to taste with sea salt and freshly ground black pepper and stir to combine well. Stuff each squid tube three-quarters full with mixture, and secure each with a toothpick.

Place potatoes and Spanish onions in a large roasting pan, add ½ cup olive oil and toss to coat well, then season to taste. Place squid tubes and tentacles over vegetables, pour wine over, cover tightly with foil, then bake at 180C for 1½ hours or until vegetables are cooked and squid is tender. Divide among bowls and serve immediately with lemon wedges passed separately.

Serves 6

Kipfler potatoes are finger-shaped, with yellow skin and waxy flesh. Substitute other waxy potatoes, such as nicola, pinkeye or patrone, if preferred.

Use coarse sea salt (not iodised) for this recipe; there is no need to use the more expensive sea salt flakes, as the salt crust is discarded upon serving.

Salt-baked trout with fennel seed sauce

1.5kg sea salt

4 egg whites

3 rainbow trout (about 500g each), cleaned

12 sprigs of dill

12 sprigs of thyme

1 lemon, cut into 6 slices

Avocado and rocket salad, to serve

FENNEL SEED SAUCE

¼ cup white wine vinegar

1 tablespoon finely chopped shallot (about 1 small shallot)

1 teaspoon fennel seeds, dry roasted

2 egg yolks

310ml olive oil

1 tablespoon finely chopped dill

For fennel seed sauce, combine vinegar, shallot and fennel seeds in a small saucepan and simmer until reduced to 1 tablespoon liquid. Place egg yolks in a bowl, then, whisking continuously, gradually add oil and whisk until mixture is well combined. Whisk in vinegar mixture and dill, then season to taste. Cover and refrigerate until required. Makes about 1¼ cups.

Place salt and egg whites in a large bowl, and, using hands, mix until salt is evenly damp.

Rinse fish inside and out, then pat dry with absorbent paper. Season cavities with sea salt and freshly ground black pepper to taste, then fill each cavity with 4 sprigs each of dill and thyme and 2 slices of lemon. Line a large roasting pan with foil and place a thin layer of salt mixture over base, then place fish, head to tail, side by side. Press remaining salt mixture over fish to cover completely, then bake at 200C for 45 minutes. Remove pan from oven and stand for 5 minutes. Using a spoon, break salt crust around fish, taking care as crust will be hot, then, using a long spatula, lift fish onto a platter. While fish is hot, carefully lift skin away, then serve immediately, or at room temperature, with fennel seed sauce and avocado and rocket salad.

Serves 6

Thai fish and pumpkin chu chee curry

400ml can coconut milk, unshaken

2 tablespoons fish sauce

1 tablespoon grated light palm sugar

6 kaffir lime leaves, torn

500g jap pumpkin, peeled and cut into 2cm pieces

800g blue-eye trevalla or barramundi fillet, or other firm-fleshed white fish fillets, skinned, pin-boned and cut into 2cm pieces

2 fresh red birdseye chillies, seeded and chopped

⅓ cup Thai basil leaves, torn

Thai basil sprigs and steamed jasmine rice, to serve

CHU CHEE CURRY PASTE

12 dried long red chillies, soaked in boiling water for 10 minutes, soaking water reserved, chillies seeded and chopped

1½ tablespoons coriander seeds, dry roasted

1 tablespoon white peppercorns

12 kaffir lime leaves, thinly sliced

8 red shallots, chopped

Finely grated rind of 1 lime

4 coriander roots and stems, cleaned and chopped

2 stalks of lemongrass, white part only, chopped

3cm piece of ginger, chopped

6 cloves of garlic

¼ cup fish sauce

Made from the sap of the sugar palm tree, palm sugar is also known as nam tan pip, jaggery, or gula melaka or jawa. It is sold in a variety of forms, from soft to very hard, and from light to dark in colour.

For chu chee curry paste, process all ingredients plus 2 tablespoons reserved chilli soaking water in a food processor until a smooth paste forms. Makes about 1 cup. Curry paste will keep stored in a sterilised jar in the refrigerator for up to 2 weeks.

Separate thick layer of coconut cream from milk in can, then place cream in a wok, bring to the boil and simmer over low heat for 10 minutes or until oil starts to separate from cream. Stir in ¼ cup curry paste, then simmer for 2-3 minutes or until fragrant. Add coconut milk, fish sauce, palm sugar and kaffir lime leaves, stir to combine, then add pumpkin and cook for 5 minutes or until pumpkin is almost cooked through. Add fish and cook for another 5 minutes or until pumpkin is tender and fish is just cooked through. Stir in chillies and Thai basil and serve immediately with steamed jasmine rice and sprigs of Thai basil.

Serves 4

Anchovy-studded roast cod with jerusalem artichokes, potato and tarragon

Jerusalem artichoke is a knobbly tuber which is similar in appearance to ginger. Despite its name, the Jerusalem artichoke is not a member of the artichoke family.

600g small kipfler potatoes, scrubbed

400g Jerusalem artichokes, peeled

800g piece of cod or other firm-fleshed white fish, skinned and pin-boned

8 anchovy fillets, drained

1 cup finely chopped flat-leaf parsley

1 tablespoon French tarragon leaves, plus 10 sprigs

35g (½ cup) breadcrumbs, made from day-old bread

1 large clove of garlic, finely chopped

40g soft unsalted butter

1 large leek, trimmed, halved lengthways and cut into 3cm pieces

60ml dry white wine

¼ cup extra virgin olive oil

Cook potatoes and artichokes separately in boiling salted water until just tender, then drain. Cool slightly, then cut potatoes in half lengthways and cut artichokes into thirds lengthways.

Using a small paring knife, make 8 equally spaced incisions in side of fish, push an anchovy into each incision, then place in a large oiled roasting pan.

Process herbs, breadcrumbs and garlic in a food processor until finely chopped. Add butter, sea salt and freshly ground black pepper to taste and process until large crumbs form, then pack over top of fish.

Place potatoes, artichokes, leek and tarragon sprigs around fish, drizzle vegetables with white wine and olive oil and roast at 190C for 25-30 minutes or until fish is just tender. Serve fish cut into slices with vegetables to the side and cooking juices spooned over.

Serves 4

Coulibiac

40g butter, chopped

400g Swiss brown mushrooms, thinly sliced

2 shallots, thinly sliced

1 bunch of spinach (about 350g), leaves removed and washed

150g (¾ cup) long-grain rice

3 hard-boiled eggs, peeled and finely chopped

Grated rind of 1 lemon

⅓ cup crème fraîche

2 375g packets of frozen block puff pastry, thawed

650g fillet of salmon or ocean trout, skinned and pin-boned

1 egg, lightly beaten

CREPES

50g buckwheat flour

60g plain flour

1 egg

1 cup milk

Butter, for cooking

For crêpes, whisk all ingredients and a pinch of salt together in a small bowl until smooth, then cover and stand for 30 minutes. Melt a little butter in a 17cm crêpe pan, then cook ¼ cups of batter for 30 seconds on each side or until lightly browned, adding more butter as necessary and stacking crêpes as you go. Cover crêpes with plastic wrap and cool. Makes about 6.

Heat butter in a large frying pan, add mushrooms, shallots and ½ teaspoon sea salt, season to taste with freshly ground black pepper and cook, stirring frequently, over high heat for 5 minutes or until mushrooms are soft and liquid has evaporated, then cool.

Add spinach leaves to a large saucepan of boiling water, drain immediately and refresh in iced water, then drain well. Open out spinach leaves and spread over pieces of absorbent paper, then pat dry.

Cook rice in boiling salted water until just tender, drain well, then return to pan and cool. Stir eggs, lemon rind and crème fraîche into cooled rice, then season to taste.

Roll out 1 block of puff pastry on a lightly floured surface until 20x30cm, lift pastry onto a baking paper-lined oven tray and place 3 crêpes lengthways, slightly overlapping, along pastry. Cover crêpes with half the spinach leaves, then top with mushroom mixture, forming a rectangle equal in size to salmon fillet. Place salmon over, tucking 4cm of tail end under so fish is of an even thickness, season to taste, then top with rice mixture. Place remaining spinach over rice to cover, then remaining crêpes, and brush exposed pastry edges with beaten egg. Roll out second block of puff pastry on a lightly floured surface until 28x33cm, then carefully place over filling, pressing pastry edges together to join. Trim pastry to create a 1.25cm border, then, using the back of a small knife, press knife at 1cm intervals into pastry to create a scalloped edge, if desired. Brush coulibiac all over with beaten egg, then, using the back of a knife, draw parallel lines through egg mixture and cut small slits at 2cm intervals in pastry to allow steam to escape. Cook at 220C for 15 minutes, then reduce oven temperature to 200C and cook for another 25 minutes, covering loosely with a piece of baking paper to prevent over-browning. Stand coulibiac for 10 minutes before serving sliced.

Serves 6

Grilled snapper with lemon salsa and herbed chickpeas

Extra virgin olive oil

2 cloves of garlic, finely chopped

2 400g cans chickpeas, rinsed and drained

1 cup (firmly packed) herbs, including
flat-leaf parsley, mint and basil,
coarsely chopped

Olive oil

4 snapper or other firm-fleshed white
fish fillets (about 180g each)

Sliced ox heart tomatoes, optional,
to serve

LEMON SALSA

1 large shallot, finely chopped

1 tablespoon white wine vinegar

1 small thin-skinned lemon

½ cup extra virgin olive oil

For lemon salsa, combine shallot, vinegar and a pinch of salt in a small bowl. Remove top and bottom from lemon, then cut into 8 wedges and remove seeds and core from each wedge. Thinly slice each wedge widthways into thin slivers, then add to shallot mixture with extra virgin olive oil and season to taste with freshly ground black pepper. Stand salsa at room temperature until required.

Heat ⅓ cup extra virgin olive oil in a saucepan, add garlic and cook over low heat for 2-3 minutes or until fragrant, then add drained chickpeas, season to taste and stir gently for 4-5 minutes or until warm. Remove from heat and stir in chopped herbs.

Heat 2 tablespoons olive oil in a large non-stick frying pan and cook fish, in batches, over medium heat for 2-3 minutes each side or until just cooked through. Divide herbed chickpeas among 4 plates, top with fish, pour fresh lemon salsa over and serve with sliced ox heart tomatoes to the side, if using.

Serves 4

Because of their thin skin and
relatively sweet flavour, Meyer
lemons are perfect for this recipe.

109

Korean red pepper paste, or gochujang, is also labelled Korean chilli paste. It is made from fermented red chilli and soybean paste, and is available from Korean and other Asian food stores.

Spicy Korean barbecued squid

2 tablespoons Korean red pepper paste

2 cloves of garlic, finely chopped

1 teaspoon grated ginger

½ cup vegetable oil

½ teaspoon sesame oil

3 green onions, white part finely chopped

1kg cleaned small squid tubes, scored and cut into 2x4cm pieces

1 tablespoon sesame seeds, lightly toasted, optional, to serve

Steamed rice, optional, to serve

SPINACH SALAD

250g baby spinach leaves

3 teaspoons light soy sauce

3 teaspoons sesame oil

3 teaspoons vegetable oil

1 clove of garlic, finely chopped

1 tablespoon sesame seeds, lightly toasted

For spinach salad, cook washed but still-wet spinach leaves in a saucepan over medium heat until just wilted. Remove immediately, refresh in iced water, drain thoroughly and gently squeeze to remove water, then place in a small bowl. Combine soy sauce, oils and garlic, then pour over spinach and toss gently to combine. Scatter sesame seeds over, then cover and refrigerate until needed. Bring to room temperature before serving.

Place red pepper paste, garlic, ginger, oils and chopped white part of green onions in a small bowl and whisk to combine well. Place squid pieces in a ceramic or glass dish, pour marinade over, then cover and refrigerate for at least 10 minutes.

Barbecue or char-grill squid, in batches, over medium heat for 1-2 minutes or until tender, turning halfway through cooking. Place spinach salad onto a large plate, top with squid, then scatter with sesame seeds and serve with steamed rice, if using.

Serves 4

To toast sesame seeds, place seeds in a small non-stick frying pan and stir continuously over low-medium heat until golden, then cool.

Steamed ruby snapper with snowpeas

6cm piece of ginger, peeled and cut into julienne

6 green onions, cut into 6cm lengths, then cut into julienne

¼ cup soy sauce

2 tablespoons sesame oil

2kg ruby snapper, cleaned and head removed

1 lime, halved and thinly sliced

450g snowpeas, topped

Sliced green onions, extra, to serve

2 tablespoons coriander sprigs

2 teaspoons toasted sesame seeds

Combine ginger and green onions in a bowl. Whisk together soy sauce and sesame oil in a small bowl until well combined.

Using a sharp knife, make 3 cuts just through skin on both sides of fish.

Line a large bamboo steamer with baking paper and, using a skewer, prick holes in it, then sprinkle paper with a handful of ginger mixture. Rub one side of fish with a little soy mixture and place, sauce-side down, over ginger mixture. Rub a little more soy mixture over top of fish, reserving 2 tablespoons. Place lime slices in fish cavity, then scatter remaining ginger mixture over top of fish. Cover steamer and place over a wok or saucepan of simmering water and steam over low-medium heat for 15-20 minutes or until fish is just tender. Add snowpeas and steam for another 30-60 seconds or until snowpeas are bright green. Drizzle fish with reserved soy mixture, scatter with extra green onion and coriander sprigs and serve immediately with snowpeas sprinkled with toasted sesame seeds.

Serves 4

Fish sauce is often used to add the salty component to South-East Asian recipes, particularly those of Thailand and Vietnam. There are different grades of fish sauce, and regional variations; Thai fish sauce is generally milder and paler than Vietnamese fish sauce.

Poached blue eye with Vietnamese herb salad and chilli dressing

4 blue-eye trevalla or other firm-fleshed white fish fillets (200g each), skinned

2 stalks of lemongrass, white part only, bruised

4 Vietnamese mint leaves

4 sprigs of dill

4 slices of lime

Steamed rice, to serve

CHILLI DRESSING

2 tablespoons caster sugar

2 fresh red birdseye chillies, finely chopped

2 cloves of garlic, finely chopped

2 tablespoons lime juice

2½ tablespoons fish sauce

¼ cup vegetable oil

VIETNAMESE HERB SALAD

⅓ cup torn mint leaves

⅓ cup Vietnamese mint leaves

⅓ cup dill sprigs

⅓ cup coriander leaves

30g (1½ cups) mizuna leaves

For chilli dressing, combine sugar and ⅓ cup water in a saucepan, stir over low heat until sugar dissolves, then bring to the boil and simmer for 2 minutes, add chillies and garlic and simmer for another 3 minutes. Remove from heat, stir in remaining ingredients except oil and cool to room temperature, then stir in oil.

For Vietnamese herb salad, combine all ingredients in a bowl.

Place fish fillets in a large frying pan, add remaining ingredients and cover with water. Slowly bring liquid just to a simmer, then remove from heat and stand, covered, for 10 minutes or until fish is tender. Remove fish from liquid and drain well.

Toss herb salad with half the dressing. Place blue-eye fillets onto plates, top with dressed salad, drizzle with remaining dressing and serve with individual bowls of steamed rice.

Serves 4

Fragrant prawn and lobster curry with coconut rice

12 small dried red chillies, soaked in warm water for 2 hours, then drained

4 cloves of garlic, chopped

8 shallots, chopped

2 stalks of lemongrass, white part only, chopped

1 tablespoon chopped galangal

2 tablespoons chopped ginger

1 tablespoon chopped fresh turmeric or 1 teaspoon ground turmeric

425ml coconut cream

2½ tablespoons peanut oil

1kg green king prawns, peeled and cleaned, leaving tails intact

2 tablespoons Thai tamarind paste (available from Asian food stores)

1 tablespoon palm sugar

2 tablespoons fish sauce

1 cooked lobster tail (about 500g), shelled, deveined and cut into 5mm-thick slices

4 kaffir lime leaves, thinly sliced

Fried shallots (available from Asian food stores) and lime wedges, to serve

COCONUT RICE

25g butter

1 onion, finely chopped

400g (2 cups) basmati rice, rinsed

¾ cup coconut milk

50g desiccated coconut

Turmeric is a rhizome from the same family as ginger. Ground turmeric has a far more concentrated flavour than fresh turmeric – both are used as often for their colour as their flavour.

For coconut rice, melt butter in a large saucepan, add onion and stir over medium heat for 5 minutes or until soft, then add rice, 1¾ cups water and remaining ingredients and bring to a simmer. Cover with a tight-fitting lid, reduce heat to low and cook for 15 minutes, then remove from heat and stand, covered, for 10 minutes.

Meanwhile, process chillies, garlic, shallots, lemongrass, galangal, ginger, turmeric and 2½ tablespoons of coconut cream in a food processor until a paste forms. Heat oil in a saucepan, add paste and stir over medium-high heat for 3-4 minutes or until fragrant. Add prawns, tamarind paste, palm sugar, fish sauce and remaining coconut cream, season to taste with sea salt and freshly ground black pepper and cook over low heat for 8-10 minutes or until prawns are just cooked through. Gently stir in lobster and half the lime leaves and cook for another 3 minutes or until lobster is heated through. Place coconut rice into bowls, top with prawn and lobster curry, sprinkle with remaining lime leaves and fried shallots, and serve with lime wedges to the side.

Serves 6

Date and spice stuffed snapper

Extra virgin olive oil
1 onion, finely chopped
130g (⅔ cup) medium-grain rice
½ teaspoon each ground cumin, cinnamon and cardamom
Large pinch of dried chilli flakes, or to taste
1¼ cups chicken stock
1½ tablespoons pomegranate molasses
300g fresh dates, seeded and coarsely chopped
50g (½ cup) walnut halves, chopped
½ cup chopped flat-leaf parsley
6 plate-size snapper (about 400g each), cleaned
Lemon halves, green salad and roast onions, optional, to serve

Heat 2½ tablespoons olive oil in a saucepan, add onion and stir over medium heat for 5 minutes or until soft. Add rice and spices and stir for another minute, then add stock, bring to the boil, then reduce heat to low, cover tightly and cook for 15 minutes or until liquid is absorbed and rice is tender. Remove from heat and stand, covered, for 5 minutes then stir in pomegranate molasses, dates, walnuts and parsley. Season mixture to taste with sea salt and freshly ground black pepper.

Using a large, sharp knife, cut through the base of the tail to the cavity opening of each fish, to enlarge cavity, then divide stuffing among fish cavities. Place fish in one large or two medium-sized oiled roasting dish(es), drizzle with olive oil, then cook at 200C for 20 minutes or until just cooked in the middle (the dorsal fin will be easily removed when fish is cooked). Serve fish immediately with lemon halves, green salad and roast onions passed separately, if using.

Serves 6

Dates and seafood may seem an unlikely combination, but they are a common pairing in Middle Eastern cuisine. The dates that are known as fresh are, in reality, semi-dried. They do, however, have soft, sweet flesh.

Monkfish tagine

2½ tablespoons extra virgin olive oil

2 onions, sliced

4 carrots, cut into 4mm slices

2 cloves of garlic, thinly sliced

1½ teaspoons each ground cumin, turmeric, ginger and paprika

½ teaspoon dried chilli flakes, or to taste

400g can tomatoes

2 cups freshly squeezed orange juice

2 teaspoons honey

85g (½ cup) muscatels or raisins

1.2kg monkfish (stargazer) or other firm-fleshed white fish fillets, trimmed and cut into 8cm pieces

⅓ cup chopped coriander

Couscous and harissa, optional, to serve

Heat olive oil in a large saucepan or casserole, add onions and carrots and stir over medium heat for 8 minutes or until beginning to soften, then add garlic and spices and stir for another 2 minutes. Add remaining ingredients except fish and coriander, reduce heat to low and simmer mixture for 20 minutes or until carrots are tender. Season mixture to taste with sea salt and freshly ground black pepper, then add fish, stir gently to combine and cook, covered, over low heat for 15 minutes or until fish is just cooked through. Stir in coriander, then serve monkfish tagine with couscous and harissa passed separately, if using.

Serves 6

Muscatels are available, with stems intact, from good greengrocers. They have a concentrated raisiny flavour and suit sweet and savoury treatment.

Pan-fried barramundi with Spanish green sauce and clams

4 thick pieces of barramundi or
other firm-fleshed white fish fillet
(about 180g each), skin on

Plain flour, seasoned to taste, for dusting,
plus 2 teaspoons extra

¼ cup olive oil

20g butter

4 cloves of garlic, finely chopped

1 teaspoon fennel seeds, coarsely ground

¼ cup each coarsely chopped flat-leaf
parsley and mint

100ml dry white wine

175ml fish stock

450g clams (vongole), rinsed

40g (½ cup) fresh podded or frozen peas

Dust fish with flour, shaking off excess. Heat 2 tablespoons oil in
a heavy-based frying pan and cook fish, skin-side down over high heat,
without moving fish, for 3-4 minutes or until skin is crisp and brown,
turn and cook for another 2 minutes, then remove from pan. Add
remaining oil and butter to pan, then add garlic and fennel seeds to
pan and stir over low heat until garlic is just beginning to brown.
Add 2 tablespoons each parsley and mint and stir for 30 seconds,
then add 2 teaspoons flour to pan and stir until well combined.
Add wine and stock to pan and stir over low heat until smooth, then
return fish to pan, skin-side up, scatter with clams and peas and cook,
covered over medium-high heat for 3-4 minutes or until clams just
open. Using a slotted spoon, divide fish and clams among 4 shallow
bowls, season liquid in pan to taste with sea salt and freshly ground
black pepper and simmer until peas are tender. Stir in remaining herbs,
then pour sauce over fish and clams and serve immediately.

Serves 4

glossary

AGED BALSAMIC VINEGAR: a fragrant, sweetish vinegar from Modena, Italy, made from concentrated grape juice and aged in wooden barrels for at least 10 years.

BARRAMUNDI: a member of the giant perch family; both wild and farmed varieties exist. Delicately flavoured, with soft flesh, barramundi is well suited to barbecuing, char-grilling, steaming, poaching and pan-frying.

BLUE-EYE TREVALLA: previously known as blue eye and blue-eye cod. A firm, white, moist, large fish with a mild flavour. Usually sold in fillets and cutlets; suits all cooking methods.

BORLOTTI BEANS: also known as roman beans, they can be eaten fresh or dried. When out of season, good-quality Italian canned varieties are an ideal substitute.

BROAD BEANS: available fresh, dried and frozen. Known as fava beans in the United States.

BUCKWHEAT FLOUR: although not a true cereal, flour is made from buckwheat grains and is available from health food stores.

BUTTER: use salted or unsalted (sweet) butter as directed (125g is equal to one stick of butter).

CALASPARRA RICE: Spanish short-grain rice used in paella. If unavailable, substitute arborio rice.

CANDLENUTS: a hard, oily, tropical nut; crushed or ground they are used as a thickening agent. The raw nut is slightly toxic, so must be cooked before eating. Substitute with macadamias.

CAPERBERRIES: fruit formed after the caper buds have flowered; caperberries are pickled, usually with stalks intact.

CAPERS: the grey-green buds of a warm-climate (usually Mediterranean) shrub, sold either dried and salted, or pickled in a vinegar brine, in varying sizes.

CORAL TROUT: a type of rock cod. Four very similar species are marketed and sold under the name "coral trout". Delicately flavoured, firm, opaque, white-fleshed fish. Best suited to poaching, steaming and baking.

CORNICHONS: tiny, sour, French gherkins.

CRAB
Blue swimmer: Small (15cm) coastal marine crab with vivid blue legs and claws. The soft, moist, sweetly flavoured meat can be used interchangeably with spanner crab meat.
Spanner: Small (15cm), unusually shaped bright-orange or brick-red crab with short legs and distinctive spanner-shaped claws. The flesh is similar in taste to blue swimmer crabs.

CREME FRAICHE: cultured thick cream, with a fresh, sour taste. Does not separate when boiled. If unavailable, substitute with sour cream.

CULTURED BUTTER: also known as lactic butter; made with ripened cream and active cultures, creating a pleasant, tangy taste. It is most commonly unsalted and used as a table butter.

DRIED GREEK OREGANO: also known as rigani; dried stems of Greek oregano are available from continental delicatessens and specialty food stores.

GOLD BAND SNAPPER: variety of snapper characterised by a yellow stripe along its top. Has firm, flaky flesh with a delicate flavour.

GRAPESEED OIL: made from grape seeds, this pale oil has no distinguishable flavour, but has a high smoking point, making it ideal for deep-frying.

GREEN: term used to describe uncooked (raw) seafood, as in green prawns or green lobster tails.

GREEN ONION: sometimes known as shallot (UK) or scallion (USA); an immature onion pulled when the top is still green and before the bulb has formed. Sold by the bunch.

JULIENNE: technique of cutting vegetables, fruit or citrus rinds into 40mm strips approximately 3mm thick.

KAFFIR LIME LEAVES: these resemble two glossy dark green leaves joined end to end; used fresh or dried in many Asian dishes in the same manner as bay leaves or curry leaves, especially in Thai cooking. Sold fresh, dried or frozen; dried leaves are less potent so double the number called for in a recipe if you substitute them for fresh leaves.

KING PRAWNS: the most commonly available prawn in Australia, king refers to the species name, rather than size, which is indicated in their labelling as either small, medium, large or jumbo. Also known as jumbo shrimp in the UK and United States.

LEBANESE EGGPLANT: a long, slender variety of baby eggplant (aubergine).

LOBSTER: mistakenly referred to as crayfish (a name which refers specifically to their freshwater cousins), lobsters found in Australian waters are known as rock lobsters. Unlike European lobsters, their claws contain very little meat.

MAHI MAHI: erroneously thought by some to be related to dolphin. This very large game fish has firm-textured flesh with a distinct central red muscle running the length of the fillet. Well suited to barbecuing, char-grilling, pan-frying and baking.

MIZUNA LEAVES: originally from Japan; a feathery, green, bitter salad leaf.

MONKFISH: also known as stargazer because of the upwards position of its eyes. Highly regarded, firm, white, moist, meaty flesh; sometimes called "poor man's lobster" due to the similarities in taste and texture. Particularly good baked, braised or stewed.

MUSSELS: a type of bivalve, distinguished by its hinged shells. Discard any mussels that do not close when shells are pressed together, as these are likely to be dead.

OCEAN TROUT: known as sea trout in other countries; medium-sized fish with firm, moist, orange-pink flesh with sweet flavour. Suits all cooking methods except deep-frying; can be used interchangeably with salmon.

OCTOPUS: belongs to marine family of cephalopods; small octopus should be cooked very briefly over high heat or they will toughen. Well suited to stir-frying, pan-frying and braising. Large octopus are tough and require tenderising, which is traditionally done by beating them against rocks; in modern times, cement mixers are used. Once tenderised, fast cooking methods may be used; slow-cooking is also suited to large octopus.

ORZO: tiny rice-shaped pasta; also known as risoni.

OUZO: aniseed-flavoured liqueur.

OYSTERS: sizes vary from species to species, but all oysters are best bought freshly shucked to order. Oysters require no cooking, or only extremely brief exposure to heat, and can simply be stirred, off the heat, into soups and stews. They can also be steamed on the half shell, deep-fried or baked.

PALM SUGAR: also known as nam tan pip, jaggery, gula melaka or jawa; made from the sap of the sugar palm tree. Sold in a variety of forms, from soft to very hard, and from light to dark in colour.

PAPRIKA: common name of a range of bright-red powders made from a variety of sweet red capsicum. There are many types and grades, including smoked, hot, mild and sweet.

PEARL BARLEY: barley which has had its outer husk (bran) removed, and has been steamed and polished; ideal for use in soups and stews.

PICKED THROUGH: method of picking through crab meat to remove any shell remnants.

PIN BONE: method of removing small bones from fish fillets, using tweezers.

POMEGRANATE MOLASSES: made from the juice of pomegranate seeds boiled down to a thick syrup. Available from delicatessens and Middle Eastern food stores.

RADICCHIO: a member of the chicory family used in Italian cooking as well as salads. Has attractive red leaves with a bitter flavour.

RED EMPEROR: large reef fish with firm, delicately flavoured white flesh. Suited to steaming, baking and pan-frying.

RICE VINEGAR: colourless vinegar made from fermented rice and seasoned with sugar and salt. Also known as seasoned rice vinegar.

SAFFRON THREADS: dried stigmas from the crocus flower. Available from specialty food stores and delicatessens.

SEMOLINA: a granular flour made from durum wheat (hard wheat). Used in pasta-making and in Middle Eastern and Indian sweet-making. Available milled fine, medium and coarse from supermarkets and delicatessens.

SHALLOTS: also known as eschalots or French shallots. Small, golden-brown or red bulbs, grown in clusters.

SHAOXING WINE: China's most famous rice wine is aged for at least 10 years, giving it a warm amber colour and mellow flavour. Not suitable for drinking. Available from Asian food stores.

SHERRY VINEGAR: made using young acidic sherry from the Jerez de la Frontera region of Spain. Matured in oak sherry casks. Available from continental delicatessens and specialty food stores.

SHRIMP PASTE: also known as kapi, trasi or belacan; a strong-scented, very firm preserved paste made from salted, dried shrimp. Used as a pungent flavouring in many South-East Asian soups and sauces. It should be chopped or sliced thinly, then wrapped in foil and roasted before being used.

SNAPPER: ranges from plate-size to large; has firm, white, moist flesh and suits most cooking methods, except deep-frying.

SPANISH ONION: a purplish-red onion with a mild flavour. Also known as red onion.

SQUID: also known as calamari; belongs to the marine family known as cephalopods. Like octopus, they have eight small arms, but squid also have two additional long tentacles. Requires only brief cooking over high heat, or longer cooking over gentle heat.

SUMAC: ground spice from a slightly astringent red berry. Available from spice shops and Middle Eastern food stores.

SWORDFISH: extremely large fish, sold in steaks or cutlets. Dense meaty flesh, with a tendency to dry out during cooking; best cooked medium-rare. Suits barbecuing, char-grilling, baking and pan-frying. Tuna or marlin may be substituted in most recipes.

TAHINI: sesame-seed paste.

THAI BASIL: also known as bai horapha, this is different from holy basil and sweet basil in both appearance and taste. Having smaller leaves and purplish stems, it has a slightly licorice or aniseed taste, and is one of the basic flavours that typify Thai cuisine.

THAI TAMARIND PASTE: made from the soft, dried pulp of the tamarind pod. Thick and purplish-black in colour, it is available from Asian food stores.

VERJUICE: unfermented grape juice, with a delicate lemon-vinegar flavour. Available from delicatessens.

VIETNAMESE MINT: not a type of mint at all, but a pungent and peppery narrow-leafed member of the buckwheat family. Also known as Cambodian mint, phak phai or laksa leaf, it is a common ingredient in Thai cuisine.

index

CLASSIC FISH STOCK

A well-made fish stock forms the foundation of many recipes, elevating soups, braises, risottos and sauces to a higher level. While making stock can be time consuming, it is not a complex process, and the results are worth it if the steps below are followed.

Bring the ingredients to the boil, then reduce heat to a gentle simmer. Stocks should not be boiled or they will go cloudy.

Never add salt to a stock during cooking – it will form the basis of myriad dishes, each with its own appropriate level of salting.

Skim the surface of stock regularly during cooking to prevent a cloudy result.

To remove fat from stock, use absorbent paper to blot the surface.

Once cooked, it is important to cool stock quickly to prevent bacteria developing. After straining, place it in bowls with wide surface areas, cool for 1 hour, then refrigerate.

To use, stocks must be brought back to the boil, to prevent bacteria development.

FISH STOCK

¼ cup olive oil

1.5kg white fish bones, washed and chopped

1 carrot, finely chopped

1 leek, finely chopped

1 stalk of celery, finely chopped

125ml dry white wine

1 bouquet garni (thyme sprigs, bay leaf, flat-leaf parsley stalks, tied together with kitchen string)

6 black peppercorns

Heat olive oil in a large heavy-based saucepan or stockpot, add bones and vegetables and cook over low heat for 6-8 minutes, taking care not to brown. Add remaining ingredients and 2.5 litres water, then bring to a simmer, reduce heat to very low and simmer gently, skimming frequently, for 20 minutes. Using a ladle, transfer stock to a large bowl lined with a fine sieve (this prevents clouding, which can occur if bones are moved), then discard solids. Cool, then refrigerate for up to 3 days or freeze for up to 1 month. Makes about 2.5 litres.

conversion chart

measures

One Australian metric measuring cup holds approximately 250ml, one Australian metric tablespoon holds 20ml, one Australian metric teaspoon holds 5ml. The difference between one country's measuring cups and another's is within a two- or three-teaspoon variance. North America, New Zealand and the United Kingdom use a 15ml tablespoon. All cup and spoon measurements are level.

We use large eggs with an average weight of 60g.

Unless specified, all fruit and vegetables are medium sized and herbs are fresh.

DRY MEASURES

metric	imperial
15g	½oz
30g	1oz
60g	2oz
90g	3oz
125g	4oz (¼lb)
155g	5oz
185g	6oz
220g	7oz
250g	8oz (½lb)
280g	9oz
315g	10oz
345g	11oz
375g	12oz (¾lb)
410g	13oz
440g	14oz
470g	15oz
500g	16oz (1lb)
750g	24oz (1½lb)
1kg	32oz (2lb)

LIQUID MEASURES

metric	imperial
30ml	1 fluid oz
60ml	2 fluid oz
100ml	3 fluid oz
125ml	4 fluid oz
150ml	5 fluid oz (¼ pint/1 gill)
190ml	6 fluid oz
250ml	8 fluid oz
300ml	10 fluid oz (½ pint)
500ml	16 fluid oz
600ml	20 fluid oz (1 pint)
1000ml (1 litre)	1¾ pints

LENGTH MEASURES

metric	imperial
3mm	⅛in
6mm	¼in
1cm	½in
2cm	¾in
2.5cm	1in
5cm	2in
6cm	2½in
8cm	3in
10cm	4in
13cm	5in
15cm	6in
18cm	7in
20cm	8in
23cm	9in
25cm	10in
28cm	11in
30cm	12in (1ft)

OVEN TEMPERATURES

These oven temperatures are only a guide. Always check the manufacturer's manual.

	°C (Celsius)	°F (Fahrenheit)	Gas Mark
Very slow	120	250	½
Slow	140-150	275-300	1-2
Moderately slow	170	325	3
Moderate	180-190	350-375	4-5
Moderately hot	200	400	6
Hot	220-230	425-450	7-8
Very hot	240	475	9